Eco-Spirituality

Toward a Reverent Life

CHARLES CUMMINGS

PAULIST PRESS
Mahwah/New York

ACKNOWLEDGMENTS

Grateful acknowledgment is made to the following publishers:

Paulist Press for excerpts from Frank Whaling, ed., *John and Charles Wesley* (copyright © 1981); Macmillan Publishing Co. for excerpts from Thomas Walsh, ed., *The Catholic Anthology: The World's Great Catholic Poetry* (copyright © 1st rev. ed., 1941), and excerpts from Rabindranath Tagore, *Gitanjali* (New York: Collier Books/Macmillan, 1971); Simon and Schuster for excerpts from Louis Untermeyer, ed., *A Treasury of Great Poems, English and American* (copyright © 1942); Vintage Press for excerpts from Joan Bennett, *Four Metaphysical Poets* (copyright © 1960). Scripture texts used in this work are taken from *The New Jerusalem Bible* (copyright © 1985 by Darton, Longman & Todd, Ltd. and Doubleday, a division of Bantam Doubleday Dell Publishing Group, Inc.), by permission of copyright owner. Psalms are quoted from *The Psalms: An Inclusive Language Version Based on the Grail Translation from the Hebrew* (copyright © 1983 by Ladies of the Grail, England), used by permission of G.I.A. Publications, Inc., Chicago, IL, exclusive agent. All rights reserved.

Library of Congress Cataloging-in-Publication Data

Cummings, Charles, 1940–
    Eco-spirituality: toward a reverent life/Charles Cummings.
      p. cm.
    Includes bibliographical references.
    ISBN 0-8091-3251-6
    1. Nature—Religious aspects. 2. Human ecology—Religious aspects. 3. Spirituality. I. Title.
    BL435.C85   1991
    261.8'362—dc20   91-3289
                                               CIP

Published by Paulist Press
997 Macarthur Boulevard
Mahwah, New Jersey 07430

Printed and bound in the United States of America

Contents

89447

DEDICATION

To the Green of Heart

Introduction

A believing Christian may lead a fruitful spiritual life and reach union with God without being very concerned about ecology. Similarly, someone may be a good ecologist without practicing any religion or even believing in God as revealed in the Judeo-Christian scriptures. Yet there is an area where contemporary ecology and Christian spirituality overlap, the area of eco-spirituality.

This form of spirituality seeks and finds God not only in prayer, sacred scripture, and the sacraments, not only in loving service of the neighbor, but also in creation, by reverencing life in all its diversity and non-living things in all their nobility as reflections of an all-wise and loving creator.

Both ecology and spirituality deal with a common reality: the material cosmos, the world where humanity dwells together with all the plants and animals that St. Francis of Assisi loved as his "brothers and sisters." No one escapes the fact of being situated in this world, in physical, material reality. The living human spirit is always enfleshed in a material body, always a being in the world with other beings, all interacting and interdependent.

People who are interested in spirituality breathe the same air, drink the same water, and walk on the same earth as the people who are interested in ecology. Beyond this obvious commonality, they share many values such as reverence for life and appreciation of beauty. This book builds a

1

bridge, or places a hyphen, between ecology and spirituality and then explores that hyphenated area until the viewpoint of ecology and the viewpoint of spirituality merge into a single eco-spiritual vision and style of life.

Because of my personal experience in a monastic community for the past thirty years, I approach eco-spirituality from the side of traditional Christian spirituality expanding its self-awareness and reaching out for a new expression of its richness, rather than from the side of contemporary ecology looking for spiritual validation.

Although as Christians we expect "a new heaven and a new earth" that were revealed to the seer of Patmos (Rev 21:1), we also believe in the value and meaning of the present material cosmos which is mysteriously foreordained to share in our human destiny. Already the new creation is in the process of coming into being, "groaning in labor pains" (Rom 8:22). As we will see, an eco-spiritual style of living collaborates in the divine plan to bring about the new creation for the praise of God's glory.

In gathering these reflections, I have drawn from numerous sources, but I have been influenced particularly by the writings of Thomas Berry, Sean McDonagh, and Albert Fritch. This book is far from being the final word on eco-spirituality; it is a provisional effort, subject to revision. Further developments in this neglected area are much to be desired.

CHAPTER ONE

※

Reality Reenchanted

Seven years before the outbreak of the American Civil War, President Franklin Pierce attempted to buy from the Duwamish Indians their ancestral land surrounding Puget Sound. Chief Seattle reluctantly consented, realizing that resistance would be ultimately futile. In 1855 the sale was finalized by the Port Elliott Treaty, and the Duwamish moved peacefully, but under protest, to a reservation.

Their protest took the form of an eloquent speech given by Chief Seattle in which he forcefully affirmed his conviction that the land was something holy.

> Every part of this soil is sacred in the estimation of my people. Every hillside, every valley, every plain and grove, has been hallowed by some sad or happy event in days long vanished. Even the rocks, which seem to be dumb and dead as they swelter in the sun along the silent shore, thrill with memories of stirring events connected with the lives of my people. . . .[1]

The Duwamish of the Pacific Northwest, like other native Americans, had an almost personal relationship with the earth. They lived in communion with a sacred presence that they could feel around them in the hills and valleys. The whole mystery of being was present in every individual part.

3

Even the rocks shared silently in the history of this noble people. The Indians and their environment formed an inter-dependent network; connected as they were to the earth, they felt connected to something sacred.

The almost mystical words of Chief Seattle fell on un-comprehending ears. In America and in other newly indus-trialized nations, nature had lost its enchantment, that is, its aura of mystery and sacredness. America in the mid-nineteenth century was enjoying an era of expansion and domination. The land was being settled and planted from coast to coast. The buffalo were being killed for their thick hides and savory tongues; the pine forests of New England and the upper midwest were clear-cut for construction needs; the hills were excavated for gold and iron ore; the rivers were dammed for electric power. Nothing could be allowed to get in the way of progress. The Indians with their antiquated value systems had to be moved to reservations where they would not interfere with the advance of industry.

The worldview of Chief Seattle was not in focus with the prevailing ethos. For the Indians, every part of the earth was sacred. They were part of the earth and the earth was part of them. Everything was interconnected and interde-pendent. Centuries of experience had taught the American Indians how to integrate harmoniously into the rhythms of nature. Their ways were deeply satisfying to them and seemed to keep them in a right relationship to the sacred.

The worldview of the great chief in Washington and of the majority of Americans was enlightened, literate, scien-tific, and rational. They operated according to a mechanistic paradigm of the universe. Matter, space and time were as predetermined as a well running machine. Science was slowly discovering all the mathematical laws that govern the clockwork of the universe and applying these principles so as to improve the standard of living. Human beings, particularly whites, were the monarchs of creation whose destiny it was to tame the wilderness and turn it to profit. Unlimited exploitation of nature was the key to unlimited economic growth. Since science had found nothing intrinsically holy in nature, the universe had lost its awesomeness. The holy was given a place of its own, the church, and a time, Sunday, when worship was appropriate and expected. Outside that restricted realm, more practical principles held sway.

The scientific-industrial worldview of the nineteenth century has continued to dominate developed countries, at the expense of the environment and of the human spirit. Only in recent decades, with the growing acceptance of the new story of the universe which we will hear later in this chapter and with the appearance of the ecological movement, has this paradigm begun to shift back toward a more humanizing approach. Reality for the Duwamish Indians and for other pre-industrial cultures was something enchanted and spellbinding, something radically sacred. In our time—in the post-industrial age of high technology—there is the potential for a reenchantment of reality that will be in the best interests of this planet and of the five to six billion people who live on it.

The two paradigms or worldviews—the post-industrial and the ecological—are on a collision course. At stake is the future of humanity. At stake also is the credibility of traditional Judeo-Christian spirituality which celebrates the spellbinding mystery of an incarnate God.

How did the present crisis come about? How did advanced western societies become so alienated from the sacred? The following two sections will survey briefly the history of science and of spirituality in the past three centuries. Our observations will remain on the social-historical level, not the level of individual spirituality. In this historical analysis there is no intention of pointing the finger of blame but only of showing how scientific, social, and religious movements have combined to alienate western civilization from its roots in a sacred creation.

WORLD WITHOUT WONDER

The natural world kept its quality of wonder and enchantment until the sixteenth or seventeenth century. Under the influence of Cartesian-Newtonian-Darwinian thinking, nature lost this quality in most industrialized societies. At the present time, as alternative worldviews become more widely known and embraced, there has been a rediscovery of the dimension of mystery present in all creation. This rediscovery may lead to a reenchantment of reality. These generalizations admit their exceptions but provide a useful overview of the picture to follow.

Descartes

René Descartes (1596–1650) is sometimes considered the father of the new, scientific way of thinking. Descartes, however, built on the earlier achievements of Copernicus, Kepler, Francis Bacon, and Galileo who overturned theories that had been sanctioned by Aristotle and the Bible and commonly accepted for two millennia. Like his mentors, Descartes took mathematics as the pattern for all genuinely certain knowledge. He preferred to quantify and measure reality rather than contemplate and admire it.

His mathematical bent led Descartes to seek clear and distinct ideas or principles that could be the basis for a logical explanation of all natural phenomena. He found these principles in a radical distinction between mind and matter, indicated in his famous words, "I think, therefore I am." Mind and matter interact but are never joined except, uneasily, in humans. Birds, beasts, fish, and insects are nothing but machines run by means of instinctual reflexes. The human body, according to Descartes, is a machine subject to will power to some extent.

By stressing the difference between mind and matter instead of their synthesis in the human person as medieval philosophy had done, Descartes made it possible to view physical nature, animals, other human beings, and even one's own body as an object. A subject stands over against objects and relates to them as a field for exploitation and manipulation. Now the world could be understood as a collection of independent, competitive objects rather than as an intricate network of interdependent systems. The world could now be brought under rational, human control for the well-being of all, or at least for the well-being of some.

Newton

René Descartes made a significant contribution to the scientific worldview, but it was Isaac Newton who advanced it to the status of a dogma that was not to be successfully challenged until the present century. Newtonian physics has remained credible because it is accurate enough within the boundaries of everyday experience. Only as a universal explanation of all micro and macro reality have Newton's laws been found inadequate.

Sir Isaac Newton (1642–1727) thoroughly assimilated Descartes' view of matter as constructed of particles in motion. Newton's second law of motion—that change of motion is proportionate to the force employed—permits a precise mathematical measurement of the attraction and repulsion of particles. Newton was also influenced by the hermetic tradition of alchemy. From this esoteric tradition

Newton absorbed a dynamic notion of sympathy/antipathy which he related to gravitational attraction and repulsion between particles of matter.

The interaction of material objects, described by Newton in the law of gravitation, takes place in an orderly way within a determined framework of space and time. The universe, like a giant clock, operates in a predictable fashion as determined by God the creator whom Newton pictures as an infinitely wise clockmaker. God wound the clock at the moment of creation and it has gone on ticking steadily and reliably ever since.

Newton's synthesis of the laws governing natural processes shows the power of critical reasoning, empirical observation, and mathematical description within a broadly theistic framework. Newton was a religious person; he postulated God's direct intervention to account for several physical phenomena in astronomy that he could not explain mathematically. For Newton the universe is not holy in itself and not a means of communion with God, as in Chief Seattle's worldview, but is created and conserved in existence by one all-holy, all-powerful, necessary being. Human reason can explain all phenomena, or will soon be able to; ultimately there is no mystery in the world, nothing to arouse a sense of wonder or fear.

Darwin

Charles Darwin (1809–1882) jolted both the scientific and the religious community with his theory on *The Origin of Species* (1859). The idea of biological evolution had been around for some time, but Darwin—along with the less well known Alfred Wallace—hit upon a mechanism that seemed to explain the facts. Drawing from different fields of natural science and from data collected during a five year voyage in the southern hemisphere, Darwin proposed the theory of "natural selection." He showed that nature favors the individuals who make the best adaptation to their environment and succeed in overcoming their competitors in the struggle for survival. These favored individuals may become the ancestors of a new species in a process of gradual evolution over the millennia.

Darwin's *Descent of Man* (1871) applied these principles to early human history, arousing severe opposition from people who believed in the literal interpretation of Genesis 1–2. More than a century later, the controversy between evolutionism and creationism has not yet died. Charles Darwin was an agnostic in religious matters but had a keen sense of wonder when observing the mysteries of nature, especially the mystery of life. Writing about the difference between living and non-living things, he says: "No one with an unbiased mind can study any living creature, however humble, without being struck with enthusiasm at its marvelous structure and properties."[2]

An effect of Darwin's theory was to strengthen the prevailing mechanical model which saw nature operating according to unchangeable biophysical principles. "Everything in nature is the result of fixed laws," says Darwin. The evolution of a species is due to the pushes and pulls of external environmental forces in a world of disconnected subjects and objects. Darwin envisioned the physical world as an arena of ruthless struggle, a battlefield: "All nature is at war, one organism with another, or with external nature." Here was a thesis that seemed to justify the spirit of competition and greed which powered the industrial revolution.

Biological science in the twentieth century finds more evidence of cooperation than of competition among nonhuman species and even among individuals of the same species in the same territory. There is a natural, dynamic balance among living creatures in their common search for food and shelter. Species do respond to environmental pressures, but also to internal regulators in their own genetic code. Fossil evidence shows that species develop not only by gradual processes, but also by unexpected jumps.

These findings have led to modifications in Darwin's theory of evolution, but his fundamental vision of a developing creation has been confirmed. Although the laws of evolution may be fixed, nature itself seems to be in continual flux. Nothing is totally static. Everything has a history. The world is an open-ended, developing process. Vatican Council II endorsed a concept of evolutionary development: "Thus the human race has passed from a rather static concept of reality to a more dynamic, evolutionary one."[3] On some level if not on all levels, the total network of reality is moving and changing like a dancer. Evolution becomes another term for the ongoing creative activity of God by which all beings are supported in the cosmic dance and gently directed to their goal.

SPIRITUALITY WITHOUT SPIRIT

Christian spirituality is a developing tradition woven of many strands, not a fixed, monolithic system. From one point of view there can be no genuine Christian spirituality without the divine Spirit of holiness. There have been saints and mystics in every century as evidence of the Spirit's active influence. In Chapter 3 we will see how many spiritual masters have found inspiration in the splendid book of creation.

From another point of view, however, several strands of Christian spirituality prominent in the past three centuries seem relatively spiritless and drab. They lack the lyric sense of wonder and of amazement at God's creation that we sense, for example, in St. Francis of Assisi. These strands merit attention in the present section because of their great influence and because of certain similarities to the Cartesian-Newtonian-Darwinian developments in science.

The Modern Devotion

To understand some of the influential currents of spirituality at the time of Descartes and Newton in the seventeenth and eighteenth centuries, we will begin somewhat earlier, with a popular movement called the "modern devotion." This movement flourished in the fifteenth and sixteenth centuries but had its origin in late medieval piety. Its most important expression, *The Imitation of Christ* by Thomas à Kempis, was completed around 1427. The first translation in English was made in 1460, and the work has been translated and published continually ever since. New editions appear even today. After the Bible, *The Imitation of Christ* is perhaps the best known religious book.

Thomas à Kempis lived in a monastery of the Brothers of the Common Life in the Netherlands. He wrote primarily for his brethren in the monastery but also for many brothers and sisters who followed the modern devotion in their own homes. Their goal was to imitate Christ by a fervent interior life nourished on meditation, reading of the Bible, and frequent holy communion. They did not stress external rituals or apostolic activity. If not anti-intellectual, they were suspicious of advanced studies. "I had rather feel compunction of heart for my sins than only know the definition of compunction."[4]

We find many sound and valuable teachings in *The Imitation of Christ* but also tendencies that later ages would exaggerate in unbalanced ways. For example we can discern a tendency to treat nature and grace as discontinuous: "The more nature is suppressed and overcome, the more grace is given" (III:54).

In what particular areas should nature be suppressed

and overcome? To begin with, there are the endless demands of one's own flesh: "To eat, to drink, to sleep, to wake, to rest, to labor, and to serve all other needs of the body is great misery and affliction for the devout soul" (I:22). Relations with others, especially of the opposite sex, are to be carefully monitored: "Be not familiar with any woman, but commend all good women to God" (I:8). It would be better to withdraw from the world as much as possible: "As often as I have been among worldly company, I have left it with less fervor of spirit than I had when I came" (I:20).

The beauty of creation is scarcely noticed by someone who is exclusively intent upon spiritual pursuits. No created thing is allowed to distract this one from the pursuit of perfection. In general, "Unless a man is clearly delivered from all love of creatures, he cannot fully attend to his Creator" (III:31).

Is it permitted to delight in any reality whatever apart from God? Only in tribulation, says Thomas à Kempis. "When you come to such a degree of patience that tribulation is sweet to you, and for the love of God is savory and pleasant in your sight, then may you trust that it is well with you" (II:12). For the "modern devotion," God was a distant, heavenly being whose judgments are incomprehensible, but who shows tender mercy to all who trust in divine help.

Jansenism

In the seventeenth century, the century of Descartes and Newton, one of the most influential religious movements was Jansenism. Although Jansenism was not a direct spiritual descendant of the "modern devotion," we notice similarities of emphasis. Cartesian polarities between mind and matter, soul and body, had a direct influence on Jansenism, as did the rigorist spirit then prevalent in French culture. Newton's view of nature as a machine with a predetermined operation also parallels some aspects of Jansenist thought. Jansenism made its appearance in France during the baroque era when it was the fashion to debase oneself and to exalt the majesty of God.

Jansenist spirituality sees a sharp dichotomy between creatures and the creator, body and soul, nature and grace. Nature has been corrupted by original sin to the point that, as Bishop Cornelius Jansen (1585–1638) maintained in his book *Augustinus*, "everything which does not come from faith is sin." This dualism, even more uncompromising than in the "modern devotion" or in Descartes, has repercussions on many levels. Morality becomes a tug of war between the "heavenly delectation" of grace and the "earthly delectation" of concupiscence which is love of self, love of sense pleasure, love of created things.

Concupiscence could be held in check only by unremitting bodily penance. Blaise Pascal (1623–1662), in his Jansenist days, wore a belt with spikes on it, because everything that appealed to the senses must be mortified. According to his sister's biography of him, Pascal reproached her for caressing her own children. Sexual love was considered sinful to the extent that one consented to the sense pleasure.[5] Mother Angelique Arnauld (1591–1661), the reforming abbess of Port-Royal, had a high opinion of women but not of men, not even of priests or monks. "She believed in the goodness of certain individuals among them, and in the depravity of the sex."[6] The monastery of Port-Royal near Versailles was the spiritual and intellectual center of the Jansenist movement.

What counted in Jansenism was interior worship and growth in humility. Abbé Saint-Cyran (1581–1643), chaplain of Port-Royal, says: "God has reduced all religion to a simple inward worship in spirit and in truth. . . ." Exterior things, including nature and other humans, were either of lesser value or a complete obstacle to perfection. To delight in a fragrant flower or in the sound of music could be sinful!

As Jerome Besoigne (1686–1763), a Jansenist theologian and doctor of the Sorbonne, explains:

> Can anyone believe that a man sins because he likes the sweetness of a flower's scent, because he is pleased by the singing of a good voice, because he enjoys the taste of some delicious fruit? I answer that if it be a matter of necessity, if he cannot help seeing, hearing, tasting, or if it has some useful purpose, whether spiritual or bodily, or is a passing relaxation such as is allowable from time to time, as pertaining to utility—he does not sin. But if he delights in it, if he seeks the pleasure simply as pleasure, then—as St. Augustine teaches by his example as much by his reasons—we have humbly to recognize that we have committed a fault requiring punishment.[7]

What notion of God is implied by Jansenist spirituality? A God who inspires fear (except in the hearts of the elect), makes inhuman demands on human weakness, and directs the course of all events according to a predetermined plan. As unchangeable physical laws govern nature, so God predetermines or predestines a chosen few to eternal happiness. Jansenists "took it for granted that nearly everybody was damned."[8] The only assurance that one has been received into God's grace is the practice of generous and constant penance. Humble, penitent individuals implore God's mercy from a distance, feeling unworthy even to enter a church. "They stand like beggars at the door of His house, but they dare not go in, for they are guilty,"[9] says Antoine Arnauld (1612–1694), an early popularizer of Jansenism.

The Jansenist controversy was entangled with French power politics and became further snarled in the struggle between Gallicanism and papal supremacy. The Jesuits entered the fray against the Jansenists, but the latter were still around when the Jesuits were suppressed in 1773. Jansenism infected bishops, priests, religious orders of men and women, dukes, duchesses and common folk; it spread from France throughout much of Europe and the British Isles. Its spirit lasted through the seventeenth and eighteenth centuries and well into the first half of the nineteenth century.[10]

What exactly was the spirit of Jansenism? We can distinguish the Jansenist theology of grace and free will, which was more than once condemned by Rome, from the spirit or spirituality of Jansenism which was much harder to eradicate. The historical reality of Jansenism was perhaps less rigorous than the Jansenist spirit which it engendered. As a label, Jansenism has come to mean a religion of severity and fear, a stern and demanding God, a penitential discipline. Ronald Knox said, "Jansenism never learned to smile."[11]

Jansenism was a spirituality without the smile of God's ever-present Spirit. While Jansenism had its roots in Catholic tradition, its Protestant counterpart in England in the sixteenth and seventeenth centuries was Puritanism. The Puritans, following the humanist William Tyndale (1494–1536), desired to purify the Church of England and lead it back to pure worship, true doctrine, and strict discipline.

Puritanism took measures to moderate the tendency to sin that is innate in humanity since the fall of our first parents. Hard work and thriftiness were extolled; dancing and similar frivolities were frowned upon. Puritanism reached the shores of America in 1607 at Jamestown and in 1630 with John Winthrop and the founding of the Massachusetts Bay Colony. From there its sober, earnest spirit spread, infiltrating the colonial ethos.

The Enlightenment

The enlightenment was less a spirituality than a spiritual philosophy, but its arid, rational temper strongly influenced eighteenth century Europe and still pervades modern thought. Originating in England in the late seventeenth century, the movement swept through France and Germany and found sympathizers among such illustrious Americans as Thomas Jefferson, Benjamin Franklin, and Thomas Paine.

The "light" of the enlightenment was the light of human reason. What human reason could prove was trustworthy; other sources of truth were downplayed as unscientific. Under the standard of human reason, these enlightened free-thinkers promoted the material and cultural progress of humankind until the cataclysm of the French Revolution (1789–1815). The revolution was the culmination of a movement that had no use for political or religious tradition and was determined to enthrone reason alone as absolute monarch.

The age of enlightenment was a time of genuine progress in many fields. In education the emphasis shifted from rote learning to a personal search for meaning. There was greater interest in non-European cultures and greater sensitivity to human dignity. Slavery was abolished; freedom of speech and freedom of the press were defended. The enlightened thing to do was to be tolerant of other people's differences and to extend a helping hand in the name of humanitarian feeling. Science, medicine, and industry made great advances and lifted the standard of living for many.

On the other hand, the narrow focus on human reason left out all non-rational areas of experience. Life was emptied of imagination, paradox, intuition, inspiration, even passion. Sentiment had no place in the cold realm of logic. In an age of enlightenment the Christian concept of revelation was unacceptable. Reason acknowledged no mysteries, only puzzles not yet unraveled by science. In 1696 the English author John Toland wrote a book with the ungainly title

Christianity not Mysterious, or, a treatise showing, That there is nothing in the Gospel contrary to Reason, nor above it; and that no Christian Doctrine can be properly called a Mystery.

The form of religion that appealed to enlightened people was deism. Deists accepted proofs for the existence of a supreme being and promoted reasonable ethical behavior as the key to happiness. They believed in love of neighbor and cooperation for the common good. Their worship centered on a moralistic sermon without elaborate ceremonies or superstitious symbols.

According to enlightened deist thought, God, the original mover of the universe and the perfect artisan, created an incomparable machine in the human person. Human thought and will are merely complex physical sensations. The title of an influential book by Julien LaMettrie was *The Human Machine* (1747). The universe is ordered by natural, physical or psychological laws without any need for miraculous divine intervention or providential guidance. God is a remote but beneficent figure completely separate from the universe.

The enlightenment fostered a totally rational, spiritless view of life. The natural world as well as the human body were understood as mechanical systems. Reason was king, and machines were its most obedient servants. Invention of the steam engine, the power loom, and the cotton gin replaced human labor and inaugurated the industrial revolution. Science promised a brighter future for all. Confidence in human ability was unbounded, and reason became the standard measure of all reality.

Since one extreme provokes its opposite, it was inevitable that a later generation should swing away from the primacy of reason toward the primacy of feeling. The high and rational hopes of the enlightenment were sobered by the irrational excesses of the French Revolution. A better paradigm was needed. For better or for worse, the new vision was romanticism.

The Romantics

The romantics of the late eighteenth to mid-nineteenth century tried to recover a more holistic view of the human person. A person is more than rational intellect; most central, most human, is the heart. Human beings live primarily by the feelings, passions, choices, and intuitions of the heart. The romantics could not conceive of humans as mere machines; instead they stressed the role of human imagination and spontaneity, human progress toward the ideal.

Romantic art is sensuous and lyrical, inspired by nature, attentive to concrete detail, aware of ineffable overtones. The American transcendentalists of the 1830s to 1850s such as Ralph Waldo Emerson, Henry David Thoreau, and Walt Whitman showed similar tendencies. European romantics expressed themselves in painting (Caspar David Friedrich, Jean Corot, Philip Runge, John Constable, Eugene Delacroix) and music (Franz Liszt, Niccolò Paganini, Fréderic Chopin, Claude Debussy). They were masters of epic narrative (Jane Austen, Sir Walter Scott, and the American James Fenimore Cooper) and of poetry (the great five in England: Wordsworth, Coleridge, Byron, Shelley, and Keats).

Romanticism was born in the midst of political revolutions and the industrial revolution. Crowded cities were blackened by coal soot, and factory workers subsisted in squalor. By contrast, the natural wilderness still remained mostly unpolluted and offered solace, healing, and beauty. Along the river Wye amid wooded hills in west England lie the picturesque ruins of a Cistercian abbey suppressed in 1536. More than two centuries later, William Wordsworth was captivated by the peace still radiating from Tintern Abbey. In a famous poem Wordsworth celebrated the powerful feelings aroused in that idyllic setting.

> . . . And I have felt
> A presence that disturbs me with the joy
> Of elevated thoughts; a sense sublime
> Of something far more deeply interfused,
> Whose dwelling is the light of setting suns,
> And the round ocean and the living air,
> And the blue sky, and in the mind of man:
> A motion and a spirit, that impels
> All thinking things, all objects of all thought,
> And rolls through all things. Therefore am I still
> A lover of the meadows and the woods,
> And mountains; and of all that we behold
> From this green earth; of all the mighty world
> Of eye, and ear—both what they half create,
> And what perceive; well pleased to recognise
> In nature and the language of the sense
> The anchor of my purest thoughts, the nurse,
> The guide, the guardian of my heart, and soul
> Of all my moral being.[12]

These lines capture many typical feelings of a romantic lover of the green earth and ancient abbey walls. The poet feels the mystic presence of a spirit deeply interfused through all of nature and within his own mind. His eye and ear respond to this spirit, half creating it and half perceiving it, for the human gives meaning to all things. He acknowledges no moral anchor or guide except nature and his own senses.

What Wordsworth calls "a motion and a spirit" is perhaps a reference to ultimate reality. For the romantics, God was immanent within nature and within their own being, knowable through feeling and sensation. The romanticist theologian F.D. Schleiermacher (1768–1834) understood faith as a feeling of absolute dependence, with emphasis on the subjective feeling. The final referent for the romantics was self rather than God.

At first glance, romanticism may seem to be an authentic spirituality, open to infinite mystery and concerned for the well-being of others. A closer look, however, reveals only another spiritless spirituality, because the romantics were ultimately engaged in a search for self. The spirit they could feel within nature was a subjective reflection or projection of human powers. The human self was the source that imposed meaning, value, and order on the world. The romantic era was unable to overcome the Cartesian split between subject and object.

Romanticism was a partial corrective to the arrogant, mechanistic worldview of the enlightenment, but not an authentic view of the human subject as an integral part of the cosmos. Romanticism softened the emphasis upon divine transcendence in favor of divine immanence but did not recognize the immanent presence of a transcendent God. The romantic movement truly valued the natural world and found there its primary inspiration, but this was not enough to restrain the exploitative tactics of the industrial age.

The world of the nineteenth century—a world of railroads, steamships, factories and foundries—was no longer the sacral world in which Chief Seattle and the Duwamish Indians lived. Only at the beginning of the twentieth century, with far-reaching discoveries in physics and astronomy, did a new story of the world begin to be told. A world that had lost its quality of enchantment during three centuries of mechanistic science and spiritless spiritualities was about to rediscover its own magic.

REENCHANTMENT OF REALITY

By the end of the nineteenth century, Europe and North America were moving full steam ahead toward the domination of nature and the exploitation of its apparently unlimited riches. At the end of the twentieth century this movement has scarcely slowed, but in some quarters there is a new consciousness of the limits of growth. There is also a new consciousness of the mysteriousness of nature and of our own place within this mystery.

The captains of industry and their partners in the research laboratories have been trying since the time of Newton to transpose the workings of nature into precise mathematical language, as if they were dealing with a complicated machine. The impressive results of the Cartesian-Newtonian method are evident but so are the grave ecological consequences of this domineering and disenchanting approach to the physical world. There is an ambivalence about this course of historical events. Without going through the stage of industrial development, western nations would not have experienced their present high standard of living. On the other hand, this development has entailed treating the world as an object of endless manipulation, and has resulted in the separation and alienation of humans from their surroundings.

The global cost of our high standard of living is enormous and will be increasingly hard to sustain in the future. There are signs that the historical stage of carefree overdevelopment is coming to an end. Environmental bills are coming due, and the present generation is beginning to pay the price. As our economic and environmental limits become more obvious, we are obliged to shift into a new framework of thought. Our assumptions about nature and the role of humankind within nature will continue to be revised until we see ourselves as part of a larger integrated, interacting totality. A part depends on the whole, just as the whole depends on the perfect functioning of every integral part.

These discoveries belong to what has been called "the new story of the universe" or "the new cosmology." This new story first began to be told in the early years of this century, by physicists. Theologians and spiritual masters did not immediately hear this news although it was a modern proclamation of the good news of God's creative, redemptive love for the world. The scientists who began telling the new story—Einstein, Planck, Heisenberg, Bohr—could scarcely believe it themselves but were fascinated by it.

For instance, Albert Einstein (1879–1955) could not accept the paradoxical implications of quantum physics, that both the speed and the position of nuclear particles cannot be determined with equal certainty. According to the "uncertainty principle" of Werner Heisenberg (1901–1976), there are situations where we must be content to know with probability rather than certainty; ours is not a totally predetermined universe but one where human subject and material object interact and influence each other, often unpredictably.

While elaborating the theory of general relativity, Einstein's own calculations led him to conclusions that he had great difficulty accepting. Like many thinkers since the time of Aristotle, Albert Einstein assumed that the universe is without a beginning and completely static—neither expanding nor contracting—although his equations did not support this view. To make the equations of his theory of gravity support a static universe, Einstein in 1917 introduced a factor he called "the cosmological constant." When in 1929 astronomers found hard evidence for an expanding universe, Einstein had the courage to revise his view and reject the cosmological constant.[13]

In the years when he accomplished his most creative work, Albert Einstein enjoyed a light-hearted, good-humored disposition, with a natural inclination to wonder and awe. It was precisely the new story of the universe that elicited his deepest wonderment. In 1932, on a visit to Mount Wilson Observatory in California, Einstein heard a lecture by Georges Lemaitre (1894–1966). This Belgian astronomer and priest lucidly explained his theory that the universe came to birth by an explosion of a "primeval atom" and has not stopped expanding. "Gleefully, Einstein jumped to his feet, applauding. 'This is the most beautiful and satisfactory explanation of creation to which I have ever listened,' he said."[14]

Lemaitre's theory, refined by other scientists over the decades, has become the standard paradigm or model of cosmology. These scientists now tell us that the universe probably originated ten to eighteen billion years ago in a hot Big Bang, the spontaneous fiery explosion of an infinitely dense and compact bundle of energy. From that primordial moment, that incandescent burst of radiation, everything that exists today has come into being, particle by particle, planet by planet, galaxy by galaxy, over those billions of years. The universe will continue expanding at a variable speed forever, unless gravitation eventually overcomes the propelling power of the initial Big Bang.

Where do we humans on planet earth fit into this cosmic scenario? Our planet is one of nine sister planets orbiting a medium sized star, a solar system formed four and a half billion years ago and tucked inconspicuously among one hundred billion stars in the Milky Way galaxy. Our galaxy is one of about one hundred billion galaxies clustering the vast

vacuum of space in regions of greater or lesser density. All
these galaxies together may be no more than a single domain
in the total expanse of the universe.

Astronomers "have not yet found a single example of
another planetary system."[15] There is no compelling evidence of intelligent life anywhere else in the universe, but
the possibility remains, and some would consider it a statisti-
cal probability.

Evidence does indicate, however, that events in the history of the universe seem to have favored the emergence of
life on our particular planet. If the rate of expansion after the
Big Bang had been significantly greater or lesser, the galaxies
and solar systems could not have formed. If the strong force
holding the nucleus of the atom together were a few percent
stronger or a few percent weaker, then stars like our sun
could not exist or could not generate heat as they do. If the
size of our planet or its orbital path around the sun were
much larger or smaller, the range of temperatures on earth
would make it as uninhabitable as its moon. If the atmosphere surrounding earth lacked sufficient oxygen or sufficient ozone to shield against ultraviolet radiation, then conditions on earth's surface could not support life as we
know it.[16]

Life as it appeared on earth three and a half billion years
ago is possible only within a thin protective envelope called
the biosphere. Human life, which emerged on our beautiful
blue-green planet about two hundred thousand years ago, is
a fragile, precarious phenomenon in the immense perspectives of an expanding universe. For its fragility and beauty,
our blue-green planet is all the more precious, and human
life is all the more marvelous. We live an enchanted life in an
enchanted world.

MAKING ROOM FOR GOD

The new cosmology, first glimpsed in this century by physicists and astronomers, has shattered the basic assumptions of the Newtonian paradigm which views the cosmos as a machine. The new paradigm prefers to see the cosmos as an emerging, organic system whose parts, both human and non-human, form an intricate network of interdependent components.

In its totality and in each of its parts, the universe is a thing of enthralling wonder, beauty, and mystery. In the words of Chief Seattle, "Every part of this soil is sacred." Each part is an integral element in the total network and cannot be destroyed or violated without damage to the whole. The Cartesian-Newtonian paradigm has proved to be a path to ecological disaster; another paradigm is crucial for our survival in the environmental crisis we now confront. The new story of the universe needs to be accompanied by a new way of thinking and acting that will be more in harmony with the cosmos.

In recent decades the implications of the new cosmology have spilled over into chemistry, medicine, and the life sciences, gradually influencing if not replacing the mechanical model. Not everyone in the scientific community has heard and accepted the new worldview, but those who have are fascinated by it and are adopting an attitude of reverence and humility before the mysterious workings of nature. Every new discovery seems to open onto further mystery. The mystery enchants and lures the observer into it.

The new story of the universe does not offer answers to all our questions. Science cannot say what caused the Big Bang or why living systems should emerge from inert matter.

Has everything come about by pure chance through the random fluctuations of energy waves or particles? Or is everything—including randomness—the result of deliberate design? Is there, behind or within the universe, a designer with infinite creative capacity and inexhaustible imagination?

The existence of God will never be proved by means of the scientific method. Yet, in the words of one contemporary researcher, "It is hard to resist the impression that the present structure of the universe, apparently so sensitive to minor alterations in the numbers, has been rather carefully thought out."[17] In similar terms the astronomer and philosopher of science Sir James Jeans (1877–1946) says: "The universe begins to look more like a great thought than like a great machine."[18]

Since a thought demands a thinker, what could be the nature and purpose of this supremely creative thinker? The mystery that enchants the careful observer of nature is ultimately the mystery of the divine creator. That mystery is endlessly fascinating! At the conclusion of his work on planetary orbits, Johannes Kepler (1571–1630) exclaimed with childlike wonder: "I thank thee, Lord God our Creator, that thou allowest me to see the beauty in thy work of creation!"[19] In the following chapter we will see how other observers and believers throughout the centuries have responded to the beauty of God's creation.

CHAPTER TWO

❧

The Beyond Within the World

Eco-spirituality explores some of the relationships that human beings have with the world around us and with God. Our environment, both human and non-human, channels divinity to us, because in every creature we can encounter in some way the creator. This chapter will elaborate the fundamental dynamics which will be applied in the remainder of the book.

A human person is partly matter and partly spirit. The embodied human spirit is able to reach out beyond all material things toward God who is pure spirit, pure being. God is the great beyond who always eludes our reach, yet not totally. We catch a glimpse from afar or sense a mysterious presence deep within. In fact, God is the infinite horizon of all our knowing, loving, and free choosing.[1]

What image do we have of God? Our image of God determines to some extent the way we relate to God. Do we think of God as predominantly transcendent, infinitely above and beyond us but always watching us from a throne of glory? Such was the image of God proclaimed by the three Hebrews in the fiery furnace who sang: "Blessed are you who fathom the abyss, enthroned on the winged creatures, praised and exalted above all forever!" (Dan 3:55).

Do we prefer to imagine a more immanent God, the

invisible companion who walks beside us on our journey through life, as the risen Christ walked with the disciples to Emmaus and "they were restrained from recognizing him" (Lk 24:16)? On a deeper level we might like to think of God dwelling within, nearer to us than we are to ourselves, permeating every cell of our body and every atom of the universe.

God is inscrutably within as well as infinitely beyond. Moreover, God is not partly within and partly beyond. God is totally within and totally beyond all beings simultaneously. Eco-spirituality takes into account both the transcendence and the immanence of God while being particularly drawn to the presence of God within each living creature and within all material reality. As we saw in Chapter 1, God's distance from the world has been accentuated in the past three centuries. Eco-spirituality brings that tendency back into better balance with divine immanence.

THE WHOLLY OTHER AND MYSTERIOUS GOD

One of the most ordinary avenues leading to the experience of divine transcendence is the sight of uncountable myriads of stars in a clear night sky. A small boy has that experience when he lies on his back in the grass on a warm summer evening and lets the stars draw him into their infinity. The artist Vincent van Gogh went out to paint the stars whenever he felt "a terrible need of—shall I say the word— religion," as he wrote to his brother. Van Gogh's famous painting "Starry Night" is a vision of luminous, gyrating whorls ablaze with energy, a vision of transcendence. A poet like Gerard Manley Hopkins found a profusion of poetic inspiration in the star-spangled sky:

> Look at the stars! look, look up at the skies!
> O look at all the fire-folk sitting in the air![2]

The fire-folk are not themselves divine, but in their silent vastness they suggest a power and a wisdom still more vast and unattainable. If the stars are far beyond us, God is the ultimate beyond, wholly other and mysterious. The transcendence of God is not only cosmological but also spiritual. Spiritual transcendence implies that God is the eternal, self-sufficient, living, personal being on whom all other beings depend and in whom all find their fulfillment. God is all-wise, all-loving, all-perfect, and the radical source of all life and goodness in the universe. God is ultimate transcendence.

The transcendence of God evokes a response of breathless awe, as when Moses heard a voice speaking from the burning bush and took off his sandals in reverence before the overpowering divine presence (Ex 3:5). At the same time the transcendent allures, fascinates, and captivates. Moses was drawn by more than natural curiosity when he said, "I must go over to look at this remarkable sight, and see why the bush is not burned" (Ex 3:3).

Rudolph Otto in his classic work *The Idea of the Holy* (1917) studied the typical human response to an experience of awe-inspiring yet fascinating mystery. He calls this response a "creature-feeling," a sense of one's own littleness and nothingness before a numinous power. Long ago the authors of the Hebrew scriptures reflected on their religious experience and realized that the feeling of creatureliness was an appropriate response to God their creator.

Creator of Heaven and Earth

The two accounts we have of creation in Genesis are religious mythology, not scientific cosmology. They teach unambiguously that "God created heaven and earth" (Gen 1:1). God transcends all because God created all that is. Until God spoke the primordial creative word, "Let there be light," there was nothing but the darkness of chaos, the "formless void" (Gen 1:2). Out of no-thing, out of no pre-existing material, the transcendent God created everything.

God was absolutely free to create or not create the universe. The ultimate answer to the question "Why beings rather than nothing?" is lost in the mystery of God's free choice. God's choice springs from the divine goodness which overflows to share the gift of existence with prodigality. "God saw all he had made, and indeed it was very good" (Gen 1:31). Another biblical author concluded that God created out of love for each creature: "Yes, you love everything that exists, and nothing that you have made disgusts you, since, if you had hated something, you would not have made it" (Wis 11:24).

The Jewish Talmud, commenting on the Genesis account, somehow deduced that God the creator practiced on twenty-six unsuccessful universes before finding exactly the right combination. On the twenty-seventh try, God supposedly said, "Let's hope it works!"[3]

Our universe is that successful try, born of hope yet fragile and always at risk of falling back into nothingness. The divine hope continues to sustain our universe unfailingly, as it conserves all things in existence from moment to moment. In this sense, creation is ongoing and never finished, for the universe depends on God from moment to moment as much as it did in the first moment of creation.

How Many Are Your Works!

The author of Psalm 148 summons all creation to praise the Lord: sun, moon, and shining stars, all birds and sea creatures, all people young and old. The final verse of the final psalm convokes all living creatures once again: "Let everything that lives and that breathes give praise to the Lord" (Ps 150:6).

Why are there so many creatures? From the psalmist's point of view, the more creatures to give praise, the more praise will be given. From a philosopher's point of view, the diversity of beings is the best possible reflection of the infinite divine goodness.[4] The loss of any species of plant or animal is an irreparable diminution. Only a countless number of different creatures can image the infinite richness of God, though not adequately. Diversity and multiplicity are signs of God's wisdom and power: "How many are your works, O Lord! In wisdom you have made them all" (Ps 104:24).

In spite of the vast number of creatures that exist and have existed in the universe, there is no more of existence itself than there would be without any creature at all. God created many beings by sharing existence with them. All creatures participate in the same existence, the infinite existence of God. For God not only has existence or being, God is being itself, and therefore all being. God is the being of all beings; but creatures, even taken altogether, are not the being of God because creatures can cease to be while God cannot. Such is the utter transcendence of God!

OVER ALL, THROUGH ALL, IN ALL

The attributes of God complement and harmonize with each another. Thus divine transcendence and divine immanence or within-ness are related dialectically, not in a mutually exclusive way. Like two sides of a coin, transcendence and immanence go together but can be viewed separately. Scripture associates them when God is said to be "all in all"

(Sir 43:28; 1 Cor 15:28). God is all as transcendent, and God is in all as immanent. In St. Paul's formula, God is "over all, through all, in all" (Eph 4:5).

Scripture speaks of the divine immanence in various ways. God's spirit is said to permeate and envelope the cosmos like the salutary atmosphere: "For the spirit of the Lord fills the world" (Wis 1:7). The spirit, as the breath of God, is in the wind that "blows where it pleases; you can hear its sound, but you cannot tell where it comes from or where it is going" (Jn 3:8). When Elijah in his cave on Mount Horeb heard the whispering sound of a gentle breeze, he "covered his face with his cloak and went out and stood at the entrance of the cave" to speak with God (1 Kgs 19:13).

Theophanies or manifestations of God in storms (Ex 20:18), stones (Gen 28:18), trees (Gen 18:1), fire (Ex 3:4), water (Ps 29:3), and cloud (Ex 13:21) demonstrate that all of nature is replete with the presence of God. God the Most High is also the most near, "a helper close at hand in time of distress" (Ps 46:2). Love and compassion are primary categories of divine immanence. "How good is the Lord to all, compassionate to all his creatures" (Ps 145:9). The author of Psalm 139 declares there is no escaping the presence of God, not in the heavens or in the depths of the earth, not at the sea's furthest end, for in every place "you are there" (Ps 139:8).

God, however, is not "there" as if physically and spatially contained in a place, but as containing every place immaterially. Toward the end of the second century, Theophilus, bishop of Antioch, expressed this paradox by saying: "God is not circumscribed by any place but is himself the place of all things."[5] God is the place where all beings are, and all are where God is, because God is everywhere. "It is in him that we live, move, and exist" (Acts 17:28).

Other early Christian writers reflected lovingly on the

mystery of the God within. In the middle of the fourth century St. Cyril of Alexandria says: "The divinity is not in a place but neither is God absent from any place, for God fills all things; God is all-pervading and is inside all as well as outside all."[6] St. Athanasius specifies that God "is in all things by his goodness and power but outside all things by his proper nature."[7] St. Hilary of Poitiers simply says: "All things are within God."[8]

In All Things, Yet Beyond All Things

If we say that all things are within God, have we slipped into pantheism? Pantheism exaggerates divine immanence to the point of identifying God and the universe. The Judeo-Christian tradition maintains both that God is immanently in all things (or all things are in God) and that God is transcendentally beyond all things.

God is the great beyond who, paradoxically, dwells within the world. Some have compared God to an infinite circle whose center is everywhere and whose circumference is nowhere. God is more intimately present to every creature than the creature is to itself.[9] Yet God is not the creature nor is the creature God. Creatures can be said to have a numinous aspect, an inner, reflected radiance, but creatures are not divine. The universe can even seem to be personalized because it is permeated with a loving divine presence, but still the universe is not God. "God translates himself into sunlight, into the plumage of birds, into pine needles and lighted windows in the snow."[10] Yet none of these is God.

Historically, there are pantheistic tendencies in early Hindu tradition, in Greek Stoicism, in certain European philosophers such as Benedict Spinoza and Gustav Fechner. However, when it comes to so-called primitive people or other people of undoubted religious piety and sincerity, we may be permitted to attribute their pantheistic-sounding

rhetoric to religious enthusiasm rather than to strictly pantheistic principles. Theological precision may sometimes be
lost in a moment of mystical insight, and language used po-
etically and symbolically is not meant to be taken literally.

For example, a Dakota Sioux Indian elder described the
Indian practice of apparently praying to the sun or to a tree
or rock. This practice is not pantheistic worship of the sun as
God but a means of getting in touch with divine power. The
elder explains:

> Everything as it moves, now and then, here and there,
> makes stops. . . . So the god has stopped. The sun, which
> is so bright and beautiful, is one place where he has
> stopped. The moon, the stars, the winds, he has been
> with. The trees, the animals, are all where he has
> stopped, and the Indian thinks of these places and sends
> his prayers there to reach the place where the god has
> stopped and win help and a blessing.[11]

The Sacrament of Creation

All creation is a sacrament, a visible sign of the invisible
divine presence. The sacramentality of creation comes first
of all from the fact that the creator leaves an imprint on every
creature, as an artist leaves something of himself or herself in
every work. Each fragrant rose or singing bird, every cell or
atom, bears some imprint of the divine creative love that
brings it into being and maintains its existence.

That imprint is the unique modality in which each individual being participates in and depends upon the transcendent divine being. Each individual, essentially related to God
by its indelible imprint, exists in the divine presence and
mediates the divine presence. This relationship to God gives
each being its worth and dignity, its mystery.[12] Because of

this relationship, the entire universe and each being in it can function as a sacrament or sign of God. All creation mediates and expresses something of the mystery of God to those who can read the signs. Chapter 3 will provide many examples of this manner of reading about God.

The innate, God-given goodness of creatures links them with the infinite goodness that is in God. "There is one alone who is good," says Jesus (Mt 19:17), but all creatures share in the stream of goodness overflowing from that single divine source. There is much evil and wickedness in the world, but beneath these defects lies an invincible core of goodness at the center of each being. The Bible contains some negative warnings about the world, because human beings have misused and corrupted the good things of this world. "Do not love the world or what is in the world," says the first letter of John (1 Jn 2:15). Yet the gospel according to John affirms: "God loved the world" (Jn 3:16). In spite of this ambiguity about "the world," the fundamental goodness of all created reality is not in doubt.

The sacramentality of creation also comes from an event that we know only by divine revelation, the incarnation of the Son of God. When the Word of God began to dwell among us, the beyond began to be within the world in an even more intimate way, forever. The Word of God is forever coming into the world "that has come into being through him" (Jn 1:10), but the world does not always recognize the presence of the Word in its midst.

When the Word became flesh, all flesh and all materiality were raised to a new dignity, a new sacramentality. The incarnation reveals God's original intention in creating the world, namely to unite the material to the spiritual and even to the divine. In the incarnation, God identifies with materiality, lifting it to a startling new dignity.

The humanity of Jesus Christ was the beginning of a

new creation. The glorification of that humanity in the paschal event of Christ's death and resurrection was the defini-
tive enactment of the new creation, although we do not yet
see all things made new (Rev 21:5). The risen Christ
ascended to the Father in a mode of existence that enables
him to be present to all dimensions of space and time simultaneously and forever. As the letter to the Colossians puts it:
"He is everything and he is in everything" (Col 3:11).

The creature in whom the sacramentality of creation is
most evident to us is the human person. Humans bear the
most unmistakable imprint of the transcendent creator in
their ability to think creatively, to love unselfishly, and to
choose freely. "God created man in the image of himself, in
the image of God he created him, male and female he created
them" (Gen 1:27). The incarnation of divinity in human nature reveals the full potentiality of our nature as radically
open to the possibility of divinization. As the perfect "image
of the unseen God" (Col 1:15), Christ is the perfect human
being and the perfect sacrament.[13]

According to the principle of sacramentality, not only
the human being but everything that exists has its own inner
meaning, beauty, and value, its own indispensable part to
play in the drama of the unfolding universe. Each participates in its own way in the transcendent mystery of being
that dwells within it. Everything deserves to be reverenced
for what it is in itself and for what it potentially reveals about
God as a sacrament of the divine presence. Living beings,
and especially human beings, deserve more reverence than
the non-living because they reveal more of the mystery of
God. Non-living beings such as rivers and oceans, mountains and deserts, deserve their own measure of respect because they too reveal aspects of the divine. Each creature is a

unique manifestation of the creator, a sacrament of the invisible God.

A Eucharistic World

The ultimate epiphany, or appearance, of God in purely material reality is the eucharist. Jesus took bread, blessed it, broke it, and gave it to his disciples. "Take it," he said, "this is my body" (Mk 14:22). Likewise he handed them a cup of wine, saying, "This is my blood" (Mk 15:24). The whole world may be a sacrament of divine presence, a means of communion with God, but the eucharist is sacrament par excellence.

Taking these New Testament texts at face value, the visible, material elements of bread and wine contain and mediate the real presence of Christ in the eucharist. Here material reality is transformed and becomes a vehicle of divine life and love. These common material elements make possible a special presence of the sacred.

Bread originates from ripe grain, and wine from the fruitful vine. The growing grain and ripening grapes draw moisture and nutrients from the soil, and energy from the sunlight. By their root systems they are connected with the earth itself, and by their stems and leaves they are part of the oxygen/carbon dioxide cycle that sustains all living things.

The grain and the grapes are raw materials that have to be cultivated, harvested, and transformed by the work of human hands before they can become elements for eucharist. Thus the finished products of bread and wine symbolically gather into themselves not only the earth and the sun but all human activity as well. In this sense, all creation participates in the eucharist. All this is the body and blood of Christ. The eucharist has cosmic significance.

On the basis of the creative transformation of bread and wine, the eucharist promises a further transformation of the material world and even the transformation of human society in justice and peace. These transformations will not be complete until all people enjoy a just share of the earth's fruits and of the products of human industry and culture.[14] Eucharist is offered as bread to feed the starving multitude, as Jesus fed the five thousand in the desert (Mt 14:13–21); otherwise it is an empty symbol.

A Sense of the Sacred

To have a sense of the sacred is to have a sense of the awesome mystery of things, the mystery which is ultimately God. The presence of God within reality is elusive; sometimes God's presence is hidden while at other times it is so powerfully manifest that it leaves us breathless.

Having a sense of the sacred does not necessarily mean making an explicit, conscious reference to God. The connection can be felt implicitly, in a joyous expansion of the spirit within. For example, one admirer of forests writes of the elation experienced in the forest in mid-winter after a snowfall when every twig and reed was clad in radiant white: "It is beauty so great and complex that the imagination is stilled into an aching hush."[15] The "aching hush" is a feeling of wonder, the thrill of being in the presence of utmost purity. Implicitly, there is a sense of the sacred.

By contrast there is an explicit reference to the sacred in the following experience. Again the setting is a forest, Muir Woods in California, but the season is summer:

A recent visit to Muir Woods occasioned a deep transformation for me. The recent rains had nurtured this special place into a wet, greening creation: rich, thick ferns, a

velvety carpet of moss, alluring beds of clover teasing me
to find the elusive four-leaf one, a babbling brook with
spawning salmon, a curious but shy deer, stately *Sequoia
sempervirens* some recording two thousand years of
earth's history, dramatic shafts of sunlight thrust into
this moist, mystic garden, a pregnant silence—and then
a sudden and unexpected breakthrough. My whole being cried out, "Who am I that you should be mindful
of me?"[16]

The cry of this man's whole being was a cry to God in the
words of the psalmist: "What are we that you should keep us
in mind, men and women that you care for us?" (Ps 8:5).

It may be easy enough to feel the presence of the sacred
in the middle of Muir Woods, but there are people whose
sense of wonder is so highly developed that they can sense
the sacred even in the most hidden places. For St. Augustine
it was enough to contemplate a lowly insect:

This work of God is so great and wonderful that not only
man, who is a rational animal . . . but even the most
diminutive insect, cannot be considered attentively
without astonishment and without praising the
Creator.[17]

Reality in all its forms continually invites us to a fuller
consideration of itself, invites us to discover the hidden harmony and order which is beyond all forms yet within them
all, invites us to dwell permanently in the place of wonderment. Is it still possible today to dwell in the place of wonderment, when we are surrounded by a desacralized and
often polluted environment?

Subsequent chapters of this book will explore that possibility. Eco-spirituality believes that the sense of the sacred is

given radically to each human being and needs only to be awakened and nurtured. This sense is not nurtured by consumerist habits of acquiring, using up, and then discarding. On the contrary, as Czech philosopher Erazim Kohak says, "You start discovering a sacramental sense when you start appreciating and treating with care even the humblest artifact."[18]

The purpose of human life has less to do with achieving higher productivity and consumption than with contemplative wonder, love, and joy in the presence of the sacred. In the following chapter we will learn how to read the book of creation in such a way as to discover the mysterious beyond within all things.

CHAPTER THREE

✤

Opening the Book of Creation

Early in 1971 three American astronauts of the Apollo 14 mission were on their way to the moon. Thousands of miles from planet earth, Edgar Mitchell gazed on a scene that took his breath away: "the incredible beauty of a splendid blue-and-white jewel floating in the vast, black sky."[1]

Not many human beings will ever see our planet from the viewpoint Mitchell reached, or have the "religious-like peak experience" he had. Yet Christian tradition teaches a way of looking at creation that leads to a similar experience of God's overpowering presence. The astronaut's breathtaking experience is a paradigm of the reverent wonder with which believers may open the book of creation to read the story of divine wisdom and power.

About a century before the Christian era, an Alexandrian Jew declared: "Through the grandeur and beauty of the creatures we may, by analogy, contemplate their author" (Wis 13:5). The analogy in question is as much an intuitive process as a reasoning process. Intuitively we understand: if creation is so marvelous, how much more marvelous must its author be! God who can never be completely comprehended can be apprehended in and through created realities.

St. Paul amplified this insight in his letter to the Romans: "Ever since the creation of the world, the invisible

41

existence of God and his everlasting power have been clearly
seen by the mind's understanding of created things" (Rom
1:20). This verse is the banner text for all subsequent
tradition whenever there is any discussion of God's self-
revelation in nature. Paul provides a rationale for valuing all
visible realities: they can move us to the loving contemplation of their creator.

Basing themselves on such biblical passages, early
Christian sages spoke of "the book of creation" or "the book
of nature."[2] Nature is an immense book written in a language everyone is able to understand. Eco-spirituality approaches the whole creation as a book to be handled with
great respect and loving care, a sacred book, the book of the
self-revelation of God. In this chapter we will trace throughout the centuries this reverent reading of the book of creation
which contrasts so sharply with the exploitive approach to
creation prevalent since the scientific-industrial revolution.

CREATION: THE WORD OF GOD

In the theological vision of the fourth gospel, God's living Word, who is God's perfect self-expression, was with
God before the creation of the universe. "He was with God
in the beginning; through him all things came into being" (Jn
1:2–3). Creation is a further self-expression or manifestation
of God which in its own special way reveals the mystery of
God. A third century bishop and theologian, St. Irenaeus of
Lyons, explains that creation is the Word of God revealing God.

Through creation itself the Word reveals God the Creator. Through the world he reveals the Lord who made

the world. Through all that is fashioned he reveals the craftsman who fashioned it all.[3]

Creation reveals God silently, wordlessly. The book of creation complements and sometimes substitutes for God's self-revelation in the written words of sacred scripture. Because God is the author of both books, creation and sacred scripture are not contradictory. "In fact," says an eighteenth century Orthodox writer, "there is a great symphony and unity between these two, so that nature is an explanation of scripture and scripture of nature."[4] Scripture and official teachings may be a superior mode of divine revelation, but creation reveals the same God, and sometimes more powerfully. Even people who are illiterate can read about God in the book of nature.

Both the book of scripture and the book of nature communicate truth. "The truth of the sunshine, the truth of the rain, the truth of the fresh air, the truth of the wind in the trees, these are *truths*. And they are always accessible!"[5] Appreciation of natural truth disposes us to accept higher truth when we are exposed to it. Until we are exposed to higher truths, the order, harmony, beauty, and power of nature can lead us to a valid, though imperfect, knowledge of God.

For many the book of creation provides the only clues they ever receive about the mystery of God. When Paul and Barnabas preached the gospel to the people of Lystra and healed a man who was lame from birth, the townspeople considered these miracle-workers to be gods appearing in human form. With some difficulty Paul and Barnabas helped the people to understand that there is only one God, the one "who alone made heaven and earth, the seas and all they contain" (Ps 146:6). They explained that the creator left clues scattered throughout creation for all to read. "He sends you rain from heaven and seasons of fruitfulness; he fills you with food and your hearts with merriment" (Acts 14:17).

The desert father St. Anthony (250–356) was illiterate, but by studying the nature of things themselves he attained spiritual wisdom. We read of him:

> A certain member of what was then considered the circle of the wise once approached the just Anthony and asked him: "How do you ever manage to carry on, Father, deprived as you are of the consolation of books?" His reply: "My book, sir philosopher, is the nature of created things, and it is always at hand when I wish to read the words of God."[6]

When St. Anthony admitted he knew how to read about God in "the nature of created things," he was acknowledging that he had reached the second stage of a three-stage spiritual journey, namely the contemplation of creation. Spiritual masters of the third and fourth centuries such as Origen and Evagrius Ponticus described three stages of the spiritual life.

The first stage comprises a period of conversion and the practice of virtue, leading to a purified heart. This stage may not be skipped or taken for granted because it opens the mind and heart to intuit the horizon of mystery in all reality. Without this disciplined openness to the sacred, a person may stop at a merely aesthetic or merely ecological appreciation of nature. Because of stage one, eco-spirituality is able to embrace ecology and transform it into a genuine spirituality.

The purity of heart attained in stage one facilitates an objective insight into the "inner meaning of created things," which is stage two, the contemplation of creation.[7] Here takes place the reading of the book of creation, leading to a discovery of God's wisdom, goodness, beauty, omnipotence and other attributes. Jesus seems to advocate such reading when he says: "Look at the birds in the sky. . . . Think of the flowers in the fields" (Mt 6:26–28). Contemplative pondering deepens our understanding of the Father's loving providence. In the book of creation we glimpse the glory of the kingdom of God.

In the final stage, called "theology," one reaches contemplative union with the triune God beyond images and concepts. These three stages are not one-time experiences but recurring ways of approaching the mystery of God. An early example of moving from contemplation of creation (stage two) to loving union with the creator (stage three) is the experience of St. Augustine and St. Monica at Ostia on the Tiber.

Talking together about eternal life as they gazed at a well-kept garden in the courtyard, Augustine and Monica "passed in review the various levels of bodily things, up to the heavens themselves, whence sun and moon and stars shine upon this earth."[8] From this shared contemplation of creation (stage two), their spirits soared "and in a flash of the mind attained to touch the eternal Wisdom which abides over all." Touching the eternal creator was a moment of "theology," the loving understanding of God beyond words (stage three).

The cosmology of that time understood the universe to consist of bodily things in their various levels and also spiritual beings such as angels. At the summit was God the creator. The various levels of being were distinct but not entirely separate; they were linked to one another, especially to the level below and the level above. Living plants are linked to the mineral world of soil and water and also to higher living beings with whom they share the ability to grow and reproduce. As historian Wallace-Hadrill explains:

It is because the fathers [of the church] see the universe [as linked parts of a single system] that they can pass in a

moment from the material to the spiritual in worship,
and back again to the material in rich appreciation and
enjoyment of its beauty.[9]

Reading the book of nature, or contemplation of creation, was common practice in the early centuries of the
Christian era. St. Basil (330–379), bishop of Caesarea, taught
the practice to the crowds that came to hear him preach
about the six days of creation as described in the book of
Genesis. He told the people: "I want creation to penetrate
you with so much admiration that everywhere, wherever
you may be, the least plant may bring to you the clear re-
membrance of the Creator."[10]

CONTEMPLATING CREATION

The art of prayerful contemplation of the book of creation continued to be practiced throughout the subsequent
centuries. In the fifth and sixth centuries the monasteries and
hermitages of the Celtic islands developed a remarkable religious culture based on the Bible and on a close relationship
with land and sea. The monks had great respect for the oak
forests and would not tolerate any cutting of these trees. A
forest glade was a sanctuary, a place of prayer for them.[11] A
disciple of St. Columban (543–615) saw birds and small animals from the forest frolicking around the saint and letting
him stroke them.[12] A seventh century Celtic hermit, Marban,
found God among "tall music-pines," in the company of
"quiet does" and chattering blackbirds.[13] A Celtic poem
called "The Hermit's Song" celebrates the monk's small hut
hidden in "a beautiful wood" beside a clear pool visited by
"an all grey lithe little lark."[14]

In the twelfth century, St. Bernard of Clairvaux wrote to

Archbishop Henry Murdac of his own practice of praying beneath the trees of the forest: "Believe me who have experience, you will find much more laboring amongst the woods than you ever will amongst books. Woods and stones will teach you what you can never hear from any master."[15] While Bernard was still alive, William of St. Thierry wrote of him:

> Indeed, to this day he confesses that whatever competence he has in the Scriptures, whatever spiritual sensitivity he has for them, stems mainly from his meditating or praying in woodland or field. And among his friends he jokes merrily of having had no other masters for such lessons but the oaks and the beeches.[16]

A Benedictine contemporary of St. Bernard, Hugh of St. Victor, talks at length about the book of creation. After quoting the psalmist, "O Lord, how great are your works, how deep are your designs" (Ps 92:6), Hugh comments:

> This whole sensible world is like some book written by the finger of God, that is, created by divine power. Individual creatures are like signs, not invented by humans but set up by God's good pleasure, in order to manifest the invisible things of divine wisdom. . . . A spiritual person who reflects on the exterior beauty of something understands interiorly how marvelous is the Creator's wisdom. . . . Therefore it is good to contemplate and admire God's works, but only if one knows how to turn the beauty of material things to spiritual profit.[17]

With St. Francis of Assisi (1181–1226), the sense of nature as a sign of God comes into sharp focus. His courteous conduct toward birds, flowers, wild and tame animals, even worms, bees and flies, is well known from dozens of anecdotes. Francis saw all creatures as his brothers and sisters because he understood that he and they had a common father, God the creator. In 1979 Pope John Paul II fittingly proclaimed St. Francis the patron saint of those who promote ecology.

Francis' sense of kinship with nature found lyrical expression in his "Canticle of Brother Sun" or "Canticle of the Creatures," the earliest surviving poetry in Italian (the Tuscan dialect). This song of joyful praise was composed under the most distressing circumstances during the year before Francis died. He was almost blind and in great pain from gastric troubles and from the wounds of the stigmata in his hands and feet. He lay in a tiny, dark, mouse-infested hut, but his spirit embraced the universe. "Be praised, my Lord, for all your creatures! In the first place for the blessed Brother Sun. . . . Be praised, my Lord, for our sister, Mother Earth, who nourishes and watches us. . . ."[18] St. Francis knew that he was part of the family of living and non-living creation, including earth, air, fire and water. It was the dying wish of Francis that all the members—male and female together—of this great family live in peace, aiding and cherishing one another.

A disciple of Francis, St. Bonaventure (1217–1274), who was influenced both by Francis and by Hugh of St. Victor, saw the entire world as a book that contains vestiges of the creator. "The book of creation clearly indicates the primacy, sublimity and dignity of the First Principle and thus the infinity of his power."[19] He says: "To read this book belongs to the highest contemplatives."[20] A fourteenth century Dominican, Meister Eckhart, said in a sermon that anyone who truly knew creatures could be excused from listening to sermons, for "every creature is full of God and is a book."[21]

St. Ignatius Loyola (1491–1556) taught in his *Spiritual Exercises* a way of seeking God in all things since God dwells in all things, "gives them being, preserves them, grants them growth, sensation, etc."[22] Ignatius himself practiced this spirituality, finding the presence of God in nature, in the city, and in the loving service of those in need. Jesuit theologians, scientists, poets, and saints down to our own time have boldly followed the invitation of St. Ignatius to discover God in the depths of all reality.[23]

In her autobiography, St. Teresa of Avila (1515–1582) writes of her early struggles in prayer. She could not reflect discursively with the intellect, but she could become recollected by looking at a statue of Christ, or reading a book, or gazing upon the book of creation.

> It helped me to look at fields, or water, or flowers. In these things I found a remembrance of the Creator. I mean that they awakened and recollected me and served as a book and reminded me of my ingratitude and sins.[24]

Jean Pierre de Caussade (1615–1751), a Jesuit spiritual director, simplified the search for God by teaching that God is to be found in the duty of every moment. Every event is like a sacrament of God's will. Every creature has a meaning in the total divine plan. "The divine activity permeates the whole universe, it pervades every creature; wherever they are it is there."[25] Creation was a book in which de Caussade studied the mysteries of God. "He moves above the smallest blades of grass as above the mighty cedar. The grains of sand are under His feet as well as the huge mountains. Wherever you may turn, there you will find His footprints!"[26]

St. Alphonsus Liguori (1696–1787) was a musician, a poet, and a theologian with a strong practical bent and an affective temperament. He knew how to move easily from contemplation of the Italian countryside to contemplation of God "who is preparing much greater delights for those who

love him." St. Alphonsus sensed the presence of God immanent within all creation: "God is in the water to wash us,
in the fire to warm us, in the sun to enlighten us, in food to
nourish us, in clothes to cover us, and in like manner in all
other things that he has created for our use."[27]

With St. Thérèse of Lisieux (1873–1897) we find once
more the explicit metaphor, "book of nature." From her observation of the differences between flowers, Thérèse drew a
lesson about finding perfection by being what God wills us
to be. She writes:

> Jesus set before me the book of nature; I understood how
> all the flowers He has created are beautiful, how the
> splendor of the rose and the whiteness of the Lily do not
> take away the perfume of the little violet or the delight-
> ful simplicity of the daisy. . . . And so it is in the world of
> souls, Jesus' garden. He willed to create great souls com-
> parable to lilies and roses, but He has created smaller
> ones and these must be content to be daisies or violets
> destined to give joy to God's glances when He looks
> down at His feet.[28]

Joseph Mary Plunkett (1887–1916) was a journalist, an
Irish patriot, and one of the planners of the 1916 Easter Rising. He was also a poet who perceived Christ wherever he
looked in the landscape around him. All nature heralds
Christ in Plunkett's poem, "I See His Blood Upon the Rose":

> I see His blood upon the rose
>   And in the stars the glory of His eyes,
> His body gleams amid eternal snows,
>   His tears fall from the skies.
> I see His face in every flower;
>   The thunder and the singing of the birds
> Are but His voice—and carven by His power

Rocks are His written words.
All pathways by His feet are worn,
    His strong heart stirs the ever-beating sea,
His crown of thorns is twined with every thorn,
    His Cross is every tree.[29]

In 1985, which was International Youth Year, Pope John Paul II addressed an encouraging letter to the youth of the world. He contrasts the influence of nature and the influence of literature, suggesting that young people are particularly susceptible to the power of the visible, natural world. They are enriched by contact with the book of nature because they are more open to mystery and able to see nature as transparent. As John Paul explains:

> One could say that by being in contact with nature we absorb into our own human existence the very mystery of creation which reveals itself to us through the untold wealth and variety of visible beings, and which at the same time is always beckoning us toward what is hidden and invisible. Wisdom—both from the inspired books as also from the testimony of many brilliant minds—seems in different ways to reveal "the transparency of the world." It is good for people to read this wonderful book —the "book of nature," which lies open for each one of us.[30]

A Scale to Heaven

Without explicitly using the metaphor of the book of creation, many Protestant authors bear witness to their own personal experience of God in the context of nature. They speak convincingly of the presence of God in all creation. As a hymn of John and Charles Wesley puts it:

> Earth then a scale to heaven shall be:
> Sense shall point out the road:
> The creatures *all* shall lead to thee,
> And all we taste be God.[31]

Jacob Boehme (1575–1624) knew that God and the world are not identical, but he affirmed that God dwells in the world and that the world is a manifestation of God. In his *Confessions*, Boehme tells of breaking out of a deep melancholy into the light of the Holy Spirit:

> In this light my spirit suddenly saw through all, and in and by all, the creatures; even in herbs and grass it knew God, who he is and how he is and what his will is. And suddenly in that light my will was set on by a mighty impulse to describe the Being of God.[32]

A religious poet who took great delight in the beautiful world God created was an Anglican priest, Thomas Traherne (1637–1674). To him the world was "Wonderfully to be delighted in and highly to be esteemed, because it is the theatre of God's righteous kingdom."[33] On his walks through the golden fields of corn, he was moved to praise the maker of all this splendor. He said we need only open our eyes to be ravished like the cherubim at the wisdom of God shining everywhere in the world, "since it is all filled with the majesty of his glory who dwelleth in it."[34] For Traherne, the least drop of water or grain of sand can never be loved too much, because "God the Author and God the End is to be beloved in it."[35] He was convinced that Christians love the world far too little, considering that God's goodness, wisdom, power, and glory are in it.

Henry Vaughan (1622–1695) was a Welsh country doctor with a gift for verse and a vast sympathy for living and non-living creatures. He looked back to his childhood as a time when he often found himself in spontaneous communion with "eternity," which is one of Vaughan's names for God. In a poem "The Retreate," he writes:

> When on some gilded Cloud, or flowre
> My gazing soul would dwell an houre,
> And in those weaker glories spy
> Some shadows of eternity.[36]

Eternity can also be seen when a full moon rises in the night sky, as in the opening lines of Vaughan's poem, "The World":

> I saw Eternity the other night
> Like a great Ring of pure and endless light.[37]

In the eighteenth century the American Puritan clergyman Cotton Mather (1663–1728) once addressed the Royal Society in London on the subject of natural phenomena as found in God's book of creatures:

> Chrysostom, I remember, mentions a twofold book of God: the book of the creatures, and the book of the scriptures: God having taught us first of all by his works, did it afterwards, by his words. We will now for a while read the former of these books; 'twill help us in reading the latter. They will admirably assist one another.[38]

A Congregationalist minister famous for his fire-and-brimstone preaching was Jonathan Edwards (1703–1758). In his autobiography, Edwards exposes a gentler side of his spirituality, a love for contemplative solitude in the midst of nature. He could feel God in a thunderstorm and sense di-

vine majesty and grace in a sunny sky. All creation proclaimed to him God's excellence. Edwards describes his contemplative experience:

> God's excellency, his wisdom, his purity and love,
> seemed to appear in every thing; in the sun, moon, and
> stars; in the clouds, and blue sky; in the grass, flowers,
> trees; in the water, and all nature; which used greatly to
> fix my mind. I often used to sit and view the moon for
> continuance; and in the day, spent much time in viewing
> the clouds and sky, to behold the sweet glory of God in
> these things.[39]

Jacob Bower (1786–1857) was a tireless traveling preacher
on the American frontier. In February 1812, as Bower's autobiography tells us, he was near despair of his own salvation.
He could not sleep for fear of waking up in hell. Then his
thoughts turned from his personal misery to the suffering of
Christ on the cross. Realizing that Christ died for him,
Bower's inner peace returned. He describes what happened
next:

> I first walked out of doors, and everything I could see,
> appeared entirely new. . . . I cast my eyes upward, and
> beheld the bright twinkling stars shining to their maker's
> praise. They appeared as so many holes through which I
> could look and see the glory of heaven. Glory to God.
> Thank God. Bless the Lord, O my soul, was busily run-
> ning through my mind.[40]

Henry David Thoreau (1817–1862) chose to live alone
for two years in a house he built by himself in the woods on
the shore of Walden Pond in Massachusetts. He intended to
live "deliberately," in great simplicity, in order to savor the
inmost marrow of life. Thoreau felt that we need periodically

to be refreshed by "the tonic of wildness," and that we can
"never have enough of nature." He had books to study if he
wished, and a garden to hoe, but he often preferred simply to
absorb the mystery of creation there and then, because "God
himself culminates in the present moment." At those moments he felt as if he were standing "in the laboratory of the
Artist who made the world and me." Thoreau describes
these times of reverie:

> Sometimes, in a summer morning, having taken my ac-
> customed bath, I sat in my sunny doorway from sunrise
> till noon, rapt in a revery, amidst the pines and hickories
> and sumachs, in undisturbed solitude and stillness,
> while the birds sang around or flitted noiseless through
> the house, until by the sun falling in at my west window,
> or the noise of some traveller's wagon on the distant
> highway, I was reminded of the lapse of time. I grew in
> those seasons like corn in the night, and they were far
> better than any work of the hands would have been.[41]

Another explorer who found spiritual renewal in the
wilderness was John Muir (1838–1914), founder of the
Sierra Club. From the majestic Yosemite in California, Muir
wrote: "God's love covers all the earth as the sky covers it,
and also fills it in every pore. And this love has voices heard
by all who have ears to hear."[42] Muir could best hear the
voice of divine love when he climbed the mountains. For
him mountains were as spiritual as they are rocky; he imag-
ined them to be alive with the divine presence. "Their material beauty is only a veil covering spiritual beauty—a divine
incarnation—instonation."[43] Using the metaphor of pages in
a book, Muir wrote to his mother:

> For the last two or three months I have worked inces-
> santly among the most remote and undiscoverable of the

deep canyons of this pierced basin, finding many a
mountain page glorious with the writing of God and in
characters that any earnest eye could read.[44]

John Muir personally experienced how communion with nature could be redemptive and could lead to a spiritual rebirth; he hoped that a national park system would make that
experience available to many others.

The Quaker scholar Thomas Kelly (1893–1941) sensed
the holy fellowship that relates all creatures to each other
through God: "It is an eternal relationship which is shared in
by every stick and stone and bird and beast and saint and
sinner of the universe."[45] Kelly felt a tender, loving care toward all human and non-human creation, modeled on God's
own love for humanity and for nature. He writes:

Not only does all creation have a new smell, as Fox
found, but it has a new value as enwrapped in the infinite Love of God, wherein not a sparrow falls to the
ground without the Father. . . . There is a tendering of
the soul, toward everything in creation, from the
sparrow's fall to the slave under the lash.[46]

THE SECRETS OF GLORY

Quotations from twentieth century authors could be
multiplied. In our century we are able to experience nature
anew through the gifted perceptions and vivid descriptions
of Aldo Leopold, Rachel Carson, Edward Abbey, Annie Dil-
lard, Wendel Berry, and others.[47] These essayists have an
almost mystic sense of harmony with all creation. If nature is
not explicitly connected with God in their writings, nonethe-

less they reverently communicate to us the mystery of nature, its numinous or sacred quality.

Our survey of the book of creation metaphor has found illustrations in almost every century. The examples are not numerous but they are constant. Discovery of God in the book of nature was never the major focus of Christian spirituality, but it was an approach that always had its appeal to a significant minority. Presumably the book of creation has always been understood and appreciated by many who have left no literary record.

For it is not to written pages that we must go in order to read the book of creation. We must put aside the written book and go out to walk the earth under the spacious sky, with our eyes and ears open to the presence of mystery surrounding us. When we are in this receptive mode, nature can speak to us of God and can begin to heal our troubled spirit. Recalling the beauty and goodness of creation, Pope John Paul II says: "Our very contact with nature has a deep restorative power; contemplation of its magnificence imparts peace and serenity."[48]

It will be helpful at this point to summarize the rich tradition we have just sampled. God is revealed in the book of creation, but creation is not identified with God, any more than the written biblical revelation is identified with God. Creation and the Bible are both word of God, each in its own way, each in harmony with the other.

Contemplation of the book of creation is based on the immanence of God and the principle of sacramentality as explained in Chapter 2. Every creature bears within it some trace of its creator, and every being is a limited but irreplaceable revelation of the divine being. Everywhere the glory of God is present, sometimes overpoweringly present. The seventh century bishop of Nineveh, Isaac the Syrian, speaks of "the secrets of the glory of God hidden in creatures."[49]

Seeing this hidden glory is often a matter of looking beneath the surface into those depths of created being which open onto the infinite. We see not only with the eye and the mind but also with the heart. Without an elaborate process of reasoning from effect to cause, the heart intuits and celebrates the presence of God in whatever is there: the wind-twisted tree, the lichen-etched rock, the twittering bird, or the endless, pulsating sea.

The gaze of mind and heart that penetrates beneath the surface and discovers the creator's loving presence is a gaze that is purified and simplified. A contemplative reading of the book of creation is more than romantic absorption in nature's beauty. The tradition rightly insists on ethical responsibility and purity of heart as preconditions for contemplative experience.

Without this ethical preparation, a person may remain on the level of aesthetic appreciation, which is valuable but is not necessarily a communion with God. Simone Weil pointedly observes: "If the beautiful is the real presence of God in matter and if contact with the beautiful is a sacrament in the full sense of the word, how is it that there are so many perverted aesthetes?"[50]

RECOVERING A VISION

During the scientific-industrial-technological revolution of the past three centuries, the book of creation was violently torn open, and its secrets were exposed for unlimited exploitation. It is not that technology is evil in itself, nor is the use of natural resources harmful in itself. After all, it was technology that put astronaut Edgar Mitchell on a spaceship from which he could see the blue-and-white jewel which is our planet.

However, along with the gains of technology has come a loss of spiritual vision, a widespread loss of the ability to see created reality as a dimension of divine revelation. The organic harmony that existed for centuries between human beings and their non-human environment has become the victim of a mentality that sees creation only as something to be dominated, manipulated, raped, and then thrown away as trash.

Eco-spirituality shows us how to become sensitive to the divine presence in all creation and how to open the book of creation reverently. In that book, as the following chapter explains, we can read not only about God but also about the harmonious relationship of interdependence that the creator established among all creatures on planet earth.

CHAPTER FOUR

๛

What Are the Dolphins Saying?

The playful dolphin with its perpetual, friendly smile turns up in literature and art throughout the centuries. In a biblical text from the second century before Christ we read: "You dolphins and all water creatures, bless the Lord, praise and exalt him above all forever" (Dan 3:79). So sang the three young Hebrews from the midst of the white-hot furnace as they gave thanks to God for preserving their lives.

Early in the Christian era, the dolphin among other fish was used as a symbol of Christ. The five letters of the Greek word for fish can be understood as an acronym, meaning "Jesus Christ, Son of God, Savior." A third century epitaph from the catacombs of St. Callistus in Rome depicts dolphins entwined around a trident, symbolizing Christ on the cross. In the dolphin's graceful leap out of the water, Christians could see a figure of Christ's resurrection out of the depths of death.

Dolphins are superb swimmers but are not really fish; they are warm-blooded mammals of the same family as whales. They nurse their young and watch over them for several years, forming extended families. Intensely gregarious, dolphins often play together, balancing objects on their fins, chasing each other at high speed.

THE VOICE OF THE DOLPHIN

Dolphins call to one another by means of whistles and moans. Their hearing approximates the human range of hearing but far exceeds our upper limits. This acoustic sensitivity is put to good use in their sonar system which beams out high-intensity clicks to locate underwater objects that cannot be seen. The U.S. Navy has even trained dolphins to sweep mine fields and to guard nuclear submarines from terrorist attacks.

The voice of the dolphin gives praise to the creator in the name of all water creatures. If dolphins could communicate with human beings, and if we were willing to listen to them, they might reproach us for disrupting their song of praise and threatening their chances of survival. The dolphins might say:

> Our sensitive hearing is painfully destroyed by under-water bombs that tuna fishermen drop to herd us to-gether. We are often trapped in their purse seines. Many of us become tangled in drift-nets set by squid hunters. Accidentally or deliberately, we are being maimed and killed by the thousands.

If we as humans were willing to be silent and listen not only to the friendly dolphins but to all living creatures, we might better appreciate how all life forms are intimately interconnected. From humans to lichens, we are all strands in one giant web of life. These strands are interwoven and interdependent in a complex kinship that has been developing for aeons. The present chapter examines numerous aspects of our interdependence.

STRANDS IN THE WEB OF LIFE

St. Paul uses the metaphor of the body of Christ to describe the Christian church. Each member has a part to play in the whole body, and the body depends on the smooth functioning of all its members. What Paul says of the church can be extended to the totality of living beings on this planet. Humans and non-humans together form an organic, interdependent whole that exists in a graceful balance. Humans may not say to the dolphins or to any creature, "We have no need of you," any more than the eye can say to the ear, "I have no need of you."

According to St. Paul, each part of the whole is expected to show concern for all the others. "If one part is hurt, all the parts share its pain. And if one part is honored, all the parts share its joy" (1 Cor 12:26). The weakest parts of the system —the animals and plants—deserve to be valued by those who are greatest in dignity, human beings, because the weakest ones prove to be "the indispensable ones" (1 Cor 12:22). Without them we could not survive.

In the Cartesian-Newtonian consciousness prevalent since the seventeenth century, the world was viewed as a collection of separate, independent entities. These could interact according to fixed laws, in a disconnected way. Contemporary western culture still operates from the assumption that the separate individual self has value in and of itself quite apart from other individuals. To speak of interdependence goes against the strong current of privatization in our culture.

However, as we saw in Chapter 1, the new story of the universe now being told by science views the world in a more holistic, integrated way. All living and non-living realities compose an organized, interlocking system. All components interact through processes that have ripple effects over the entire network. Each component of the system lives off the surplus generated lower on the food chain, and in turn generates a surplus to feed higher life forms. In the long run, all are essentially dependent on all others. The individual survives and thrives if the entire ecosystem thrives.

To illustrate the extent to which life forms interdepend and even participate in one another biophysically, Ken Wilber explains:

> Ninety-eight percent of our body's atoms are replaced annually. Each time we breathe, we take in a quadrillion atoms breathed by the rest of the human race within the past two weeks . . . even while we live, we are constantly returning to earth, constantly engaged in a tremendous exchange, a cooperative partnership. . . .[1]

Each living individual subsists by a constant process of giving to and receiving from others. The atoms that constitute a particular life form at a particular moment will circulate to constitute another life form at another moment, without prejudice to the unity of either. By breathing and eating, living beings physically incorporate and participate in the whole cosmos.

The cosmos resembles the orderly unity of a living, acting being more than the juxtaposition of parts in a giant machine. Living and non-living components depend on one another in a network of relationships. The whole interconnected network is in constant, dynamic flux: from the activity of particles within the atom, to the firing of nerve cells in a human brain, to the rotation of galaxies and star clusters in outer space.

The finely-tuned design of the cosmos depends upon the divine designer. "How lovely, all his works, how dazzling to the eye! . . . All things go by pairs, by opposites; he has not made anything imperfect: one thing complements the excellence of another. Who could ever grow tired of gazing at his glory?" (Sir 43:22–25). Dependence upon God and upon other creatures does not diminish human dignity or human freedom. God is not a despotic designer who feels threatened by any signs of initiative on our part. Instead, God empowers us to exercise freely our creative capacities. We depend on God "as living beings depend on the sun for life-nourishing possibilities."[2]

ENDANGERED SPECIES

In the interlocking totality of sentient beings, humans are but one species, although greatest in dignity, within the entire community of life forms. So far, humans have not been put on the list of endangered species, but the list is crowded with hundreds of other threatened creatures. According to World Wildlife Fund estimates in 1989, about four hundred species of plants and animals are disappearing each year. When an entire species is extinct, there is no way to resurrect it. The passenger pigeon and the Carolina parakeet will never fly again.

Similarly, when a fragile ecosystem such as a tropical rain forest is destroyed, it cannot ever be put back together again; reassembling Humpty Dumpty would be far easier. Because of interdependence, the harm done to a rain forest spreads globally: the increased levels of carbon dioxide in the atmosphere further erode the ozone layer, exposing the planet to more ultraviolet radiation and aggravating the "greenhouse effect" of global warming. Radiant heat cannot escape through the carbon dioxide blanket covering the earth. Destruction of the habitat for insects, birds, and animals means less biodiversity. Destruction of plants could mean depletion of sources for new medicines and chemicals. When a forest is lost, everybody eventually loses. The entire community of beings stands in solidarity, for loss or for gain.

Sharing one planet, the worldwide community of beings is endangered if the air, water, and soil are threatened. When the air is polluted, the water contaminated with chemicals, and the fertile topsoil eroded away, then no one enjoys a healthy quality of life. Today there are still pockets of healthful environment left here and there, but future generations may not find so many. Concern for the well-being of future generations and of the planet is an essential ethical consideration in eco-spirituality.

FEELING AT HOME

Eco-spirituality is a spirituality of feeling at home in our own house. The word "ecology" comes from Greek words meaning talk about one's house, one's surroundings. If we fail to understand the house in which we live, feel at home in it, and treat it respectfully, we are likely to bring the whole house down around our ears.

We live in many houses simultaneously. We live in the house which is our body. Thus it is part of a sound eco-spirituality to feel at home in our body, to live in harmony with the world of our own person. We safeguard personal wellness through a balanced regimen of exercise, rest, and diet, avoiding substance abuse and other excesses. Eco-spirituality is holistic, not dualistic as in the Cartesian paradigm. We do not regard the flesh as evil or degrading, as in the Manichaean view. We see persons as embodied spirits or inspirited bodies. Spirit and body are interdependent; there is no saving the soul without the body.[3]

We also live in the house which is our dwelling place,

our family household. This household is situated in a particular bioregion. Bioregions are geographically defined regions
such as coastal lowlands, intermountain plains, river water-
sheds, and high desert areas. Bioregions have their own
flora, fauna, and climatic conditions, their own appropriate
economy, sometimes their own language and culture. These
regions often overrun arbitrary state and national boundaries. Interdependence is strong within each bioregion, and
bioregions also depend on one another.[4] One region may be
dependent on energy sources outside its boundaries, while
supplying necessary minerals to another region.

Eco-spirituality fosters a certain bioregional loyalty, the
feeling of being at home within one's bioregion, being in
communion with one's proximate environment. On this
level, the concern would be to prevent or reduce pollution of
our bioregion and to capitalize on its resources while living
within its physical limitations.

Extending the notion of house to another degree, we
find ourselves living in the immense house which is planet
earth. Eco-spirituality teaches us to live peacefully in our
earth home and to let all other beings live with us as neighbors. We depend on one another; our existences are insepara-
bly intertwined. The more we live in harmony with the other
inhabitants of this house, the more we can all feel at home.
Northern and southern hemispheres need to co-exist as
equal partners, now that east-west tensions have been
reduced.

Earth is not our permanent home, for "there is no permanent city for us here" (Heb 13:14), but this planet is all we
have for as long as we live here. It is our responsibility to
leave behind us a viable, habitable home for future generations. The human potentiality for seriously damaging this
planet is formidable, even apart from the prospect of a nuclear war followed by a nuclear winter. Nuclear war is only a

quicker path to the environmental wasteland which we are now creating by our reckless exploitation of the earth's non-renewable resources such as fossil fuels.

Until recent decades, it was generally accepted that humanity has a God-given right to exploit the earth without limit. Did not God say to the first humans: "Be fruitful, multiply, fill the earth and subdue it. Be masters of the fish of the sea, the birds of heaven and all the living creatures that move on earth" (Gen 1:28)? What precisely is the meaning of this biblical mandate in the context of a world that is a network of socially and physically interdependent beings?

FAITHFUL CARETAKER

There have been several attempts to reinterpret what Genesis says about subduing and mastering the earth. Interpretations that would justify unrestricted exploitation are no longer fashionable. As ecologist Jeremy Rifkin puts it: "We have misread our mandate. We believed that to have dominion meant to exert power, to control, to dominate."[5] Domination was a typically masculine or patriarchal explanation. Domination has led us to devastation.

However, it must be admitted that the supposed right to dominate nature was highly favorable to the development of the sciences. For centuries, science and industry have viewed the world as an object to be utilized and manipulated for human benefit. Humanity does possess an unchallenged right to use the goods of the earth, but use has too often become abuse. Although the benefits are undeniable, in many cases the side-effects of industrialized agriculture and economic development now outweigh the benefits. Down this avenue lies further devastation of land, air, and water.

Therefore some would prefer to say the role of humans

is to provide good management of God's creation: oversee-ing and directing natural processes, keeping everything in order, and making good the defects of nature by energetic managerial interventions in the environment. The goal would be scientific management of the earth's resources for the benefit of all.

However, this managerial model responds to nature from the position of an outsider more than a participant in the process. It is possible to manage an isolated garden or a farm fairly well, but it is quite unrealistic to think of manag-ing the intricate ecosystem of the whole planet in which hu-mans are participants. According to David Ehrenfeld, "In no important instance have we been able to demonstrate com-prehensive, successful management of our world, nor do we understand it well enough to be able to manage it in theory."[6]

A somewhat better model is stewardship. Humans are not the managers of this world but the stewards, agents, or trustees of God, charged with the safekeeping of the world's resources for the benefit of all. Jesus praised the wise and trustworthy steward who gave his household their allow-ance of food at the proper time (Lk 12:42). In the same con-text, Jesus pointed out the danger of a steward growing care-less or being concerned only for his own welfare. As stewards we are responsible for maintaining the integrity of the earth and will have to give an account to God of how we have used or abused our position. "Draw me up an account of your stewardship," says the master in a parable told by Jesus, "because you are not to be my steward any longer" (Lk 16:2).

The stewardship model is ambivalent, for there are dis-honest as well as honest stewards. A steward's position in-cludes high potential for mismanagement, but in its best sense the steward's role is wisely to foster the unfolding of the master's plan for the whole household.

If the term "steward" seems too ambivalent, perhaps the proper role of humans on earth is that of faithful caretaker. The caretaker model incorporates the best features of the stewardship model and adds the quality of faithful, loving care. The caretaker never exploits, never acts like a tyrant. The caretaker is not the owner but the guardian. God is the owner, the maker: "To him belongs the sea, for he made it, and the dry land shaped by his hands" (Ps 95:4). The caretaker's task is to nurture, heal, and restore, fostering life and harmony everywhere.

God has appointed humans to be the faithful caretakers of God's garden which is this world. The alienation and strife brought into the world by sin did not abolish our mandate to be caretaker or guardian of God's garden, but made it more difficult to accomplish the task. Human beings remain the caretakers of creation because only we are made according to the image of God (Gen 1:27). As caretakers reflecting the divine image, we are called to mirror God's own way of acting and to cooperate creatively and lovingly in the plan of God who is creator, redeemer, and sustainer of all. As God's plan unfolds, with human cooperation, the world that is degraded and enslaved will slowly be set free and transformed into a glorious new creation (Rom 8:21).

In the caretaker interpretation of "subdue the earth" (Gen 1:27), human beings are people who care about the earth and its resources, and care for the whole network of interdependent beings. For a caretaker the issue is not mastery or control but harmony. A caretaker does not impose order from outside but from within, guarding the existing integrity of the whole interdependent system.

The world is not a haphazard jumble of random energy

and matter that need to be organized but a harmoniously organized whole that includes human beings as parts of the whole. Although we human caretakers rank first in dignity because of our God-given transcendence over other beings, we do need to listen to others, listen to the dolphins and to all other creatures, with docility and respect.

SHEPHERD OF BEINGS

Humanity is the shepherd of these myriad beings. The role of humanity as shepherd is to tend the whole flock of beings, to take loving care of them. A shepherd who is a good shepherd knows the sheep and respects their individuality as much as possible. Considering the sheer number of human and non-human beings, our responsibility on this earth is awesome.

The task is not, however, hopeless, because in this plurality of beings there is an amazing order. Each component, living and non-living, occupies its appropriate niche or level. Between levels, the rule is cooperation more often than competition. Even competition for food and territory takes place within a larger context of cooperation.

The levels seem to be organized in a hierarchical way, so that the higher includes the lower while transcending it. Ken Wilber explains:

> That is, all of the lower is "in" the highest, but not all the higher is in the lower. As a simple example, there is a sense in which all of the reptile is in the man, but not all the man is in the reptile, all of the mineral world is in a plant, but not vice versa, and so on.[7]

The place of human beings in this integrated, hierarchically structured complex has been described by saying that a human being is a microcosm of the surrounding macro-cosm.[8] That is, humans sum up and recapitulate the various levels of being—mineral, vegetable, animal, and spiritual—that are found in the macrocosm. "We are made both of the dust of the earth and of the breath of God, united in a single person."[9] The human fetus must go through successive stages of development that parallel many non-human forms until the human form is ultimately attained.

The vital rhythms that move the seasons and the oceans, the atoms and the stars, can all be felt within the microcosm of the human heart. Bengali poet and playwright Rabindranath Tagore writes of the stream of life flowing through microcosm and macrocosm:

> The same stream of life that runs through my veins night and day runs through the world and dances in rhythmic measures.
> It is the same life that shoots in joy through the dust of the earth in numberless blades of grass and breaks into tumultuous waves of leaves and flowers.
> It is the same life that is rocked in the ocean-cradle of birth and of death, in ebb and in flow.
> I feel my limbs are made glorious by the touch of this world of life, and my pride is from the life-throb of ages dancing in my blood this moment.[10]

In his roles of caretaker and shepherd of all created be-ings, the poet celebrates the throbbing stream of life that sustains us and binds us together. Humans serve as the con-sciousness of the cosmos. Thomas Berry, who has been called a "geologian," says that a human person is "that being in whom the universe reflects on and celebrates itself in conscious self-awareness."[11]

In the cave art and petroglyphs left by prehistoric humans we have exquisite depictions of the animals which they hunted or perhaps domesticated. Our forebears felt a kind of kinship with these creatures on whom they depended for their livelihood. They survived by living in harmony with nature, shepherding its multiple resources and celebrating its bounty.

The ancient author of Psalm 104 celebrates the vital interdependence of wind and rainfall, birds of heaven, cedar trees and growing grass, the sea vast and wide, beasts of the field and forest, and human beings. All of these depend on one another and on God: "All of these look to you to give them their food in due season" (Ps 104:27). According to biblical scholar M. Weiss, the psalmist was describing the bonds of mutual helpfulness that connect the creator and all creatures: "Our poet does not, then, see the phenomena of nature in isolation from one another, but rather in their interrelationship."[12]

ENRICHING DIVERSITY

Eco-spirituality recognizes, as did Thomas Merton listening to the nightly chorus of frogs outside his hermitage, that "Only as part of the world's fabric and dynamism can I find my true being in God, who has willed me to exist in the world."[13] When Merton lived in the monastery, the frogs kept him awake at night. In the hermitage, however, "They do not keep me awake; they are a comfort, an extension of my own being."

To appreciate other creatures as an extension of one's own being implies a deep identification with the basic goodness of nature. Someone who can be inspired rather than annoyed by a chorus of croaking frogs is open to goodness and beauty wherever they may be found. Listening to the song of the frogs requires at least as much patience as listening to dolphins, but the songs of all these creatures can be perceived as songs of praise to the creator.

In fact, the theological reason for the plurality and diversity of created beings is multiplication of the creator's praise. No single creature could adequately represent the infinite perfection and goodness of God. Taken all together in a colossal chorus of praise, the multitude of creatures glorifies God more perfectly than could any individual alone. As St. Thomas Aquinas teaches: "The whole universe together participates the divine goodness more perfectly, and represents it better than any single creature whatever."[14]

God made countless millions of different beings to reveal the divine goodness and wisdom. "How many are your works, O Lord! In wisdom you have made them all" (Ps 104:24). Wisdom is personified as the collaborator in the work of creation, or as a playful child, the darling of Yahweh. "I was beside the master craftsman, delighting him day after day, ever at play in his presence, at play everywhere on his earth" (Prov 8:30–31).

Wisdom's playfulness is reflected in those extravagant creatures called Behemoth and Leviathan in the book of Job (Job 40:15–32) that seem to have been made just for the fun of it, to show what can be done by an omnipotent, imaginative artist. In the words of the nineteenth century naturalist, Louis Agassiz: "The possibilities of existence run so deeply into the extravagant that there is scarcely any conception too extraordinary for Nature to realize."[15]

The plurality of creatures is beneficial because they relate to one another in basically cooperative ways. Each functions according to its own uniqueness, making a distinctive contribution to the whole and receiving its further meaning from the whole. A system restricted to a single life form, a monoculture, is vulnerable to swift destruction because it lacks the options and flexibility of a more diverse system. Ecologist John Livingston explains: "The concept of a healthy ecosystem is one with many parts, many roles, many inter-relationships, many alternatives, many structures and functions, many ways of doing things."[16]

Biological diversity enriches the ecological balance of plant and animal life within each bioregion. Among the multitudes of life forms there is overall harmony and inter-dependence. Diversity is nature's polyphony. Yet how could we close our eyes and ears to the many dissonant and absurd elements in nature? In place of harmonious diversity we often find situations of chaos brought about by natural disasters and by human carelessness or incompetence.

We take the predominant good order of nature too much for granted and are surprised by evidence of chaos. Yet it is not chaos that should surprise us but the God-given order and design of the whole universe.[17] The stability and regularity of natural processes are highly improbable if the second law of thermodynamics always holds true. That law, called the principle of entropy, postulates a tendency in every isolated or closed system toward disorder, loss of heat, and eventual lifelessness.

However, in particular open, non-isolated conditions we do see order spontaneously arising out of chaos, according to the 1977 Nobel Prize chemist Ilya Prigogine.[18] And new life rises from the chaos of death, according to Christian belief in the paschal mystery. Death is the moment of rebirth. As the poet Francis Thompson puts it: "For there is nothing lives but something dies, And there is nothing dies but something lives."[19]

Still, it requires an input of energy or effort from some source to resist the forces of disorder. Instead of resisting disorder, human enterprise has been accelerating disorder in many parts of the ecosystem. Any activity that disrupts the harmony and shatters the balance of nature is working counter to our primal mandate to care for the earth and shepherd all beings. Instead, humans ought to be working together to preserve the integrity of creation and to tend the variegated community of beings.

UNITY AND PEACE

Even in a world as interdependent as ours, unity does not come easily and is not easily maintained. Is it really possible to transcend the radical polarities we experience between human and non-human, body and spirit, male and female, white and non-white, conservation and development? Can these tensions be integrated creatively into a single, harmonious, world-community at peace with itself, with the environment, and with God?

Eco-spirituality realizes that it may take more than human good will to achieve this vision of a unity that embraces and celebrates diversity, finding all things in God and God in all things. Ultimately it will be the power of God, the Holy Spirit, that brings the divergent parts together and lovingly binds them into one. From the Spirit, says Sean McDonagh, a missionary in the Philippines, "comes the great urge to heal what is broken, re-unite what is separated, and recreate the face of the earth."[20]

The Spirit of God is the principle of unity who reconnects all things. Creating unity out of diversity is a work of the Spirit of love. Only the love that overcomes fear can open ears to hear the other and open minds to understand the other. With listening and understanding will come sharing. With sharing will come compassion and appreciation, and eventually a new creation.

The new creation, promised by the Hebrew prophets (Is

65:17; 66:22) is already inaugurated in the new covenant. The Holy Spirit released on Pentecost is the principle of a new communal reality that is drawing all things together into one under Jesus Christ as head (Eph 1:10). No living thing is to be excluded: "When that day comes I shall make a covenant for them with the wild animals, with the birds of heaven and the creeping things of the earth" (Hos 2:20). This new covenant is to be as inclusive and all-embracing as the covenant God made with Noah after the flood, which was "an eternal covenant between God and every living creature on earth, that is, all living things" (Gen 9:16). The memorial sign of the covenant with Noah is the rainbow which envelops the earth and all creatures in its colorful curve.

The Judeo-Christian expectation of the new creation includes peace between humans and wild animals. Isaiah's prophecy says:

> The wolf will live with the lamb, the panther lie down with the kid, calf, lion and fat-stock beast together, with a little boy to lead them. The cow and the bear will graze, their young will lie down together. The lion will eat hay like the ox. The infant will play over the den of the adder; the baby will put his hand into the viper's lair (Is 11:6–9).

Although the details of such prophecies need not be taken literally, tradition does record some remarkable examples of peace between humans and animals. When Jesus spent forty days in the desert, "he was with the wild animals" but was unharmed (Mk 1:13). St. Paul was gathering sticks for a fire after being shipwrecked off Malta, "when a viper brought out by the heat attached itself to his hand," but he came to no harm (Acts 28:3).

There is an anecdote about St. Macarius who lived in a

cave in the Egyptian desert in the fourth century. His prayers restored sight to hyena cubs that had been born blind, after the mother hyena persuaded Macarius to come to her den by licking his feet and then "taking him gently by the hem of his tunic."[21] In another story from monastic tradition, Abba Gerasimus encountered a lion while walking along the bank of the Jordan River. The lion was roaring with pain because it had a festering thorn in its paw. When the lion noticed Abba Gerasimus, it held out its wounded paw, whining and begging the old monk to treat it. Gerasimus sat down, took the lion's paw in his lap, pulled out the thorn, cleaned the wound carefully, and bound it with a cloth bandage. Afterward the lion "refused to leave the old man, and followed him around like an affectionate disciple."[22]

The *Fioretti* of St. Francis describe how, with the sign of the cross, he pacified the wolf of Gubbio, an animal "so ferocious and terrible that it devoured not only animals but also men."[23] In nineteenth century Russia, when St. Seraphim of Sarov lived as a hermit in the forest, he is said to have fed the bears from his hand. In our own century, during the lifetime of Albert Schweitzer (1875–1965), antelope, pelicans, and monkeys roamed the premises of his jungle hospital along with sheep and goats, chickens, dogs and cats.

The common theme in all of these remarkable stories is that the peace that will prevail in the new creation will affect all living beings in their relationships to one another. The biblical ideal of peace, *shalom*, implies universal harmony and security, both interior and exterior. Where there is peace, mutual interdependence will be everywhere acknowledged and celebrated. Peace is a condition of total well-being that includes even the earth, for there is a positive bonding between human beings and the earth. In Isaiah's description, the desert itself will blossom: "Let the desert and the dry lands be glad, let the wasteland rejoice and bloom; like the asphodel, let it burst into flower, let it rejoice and sing for joy" (Is 35:1–2). In more prosaic language, the world will be at peace when we have minimized all injustice and "have learned to dwell sanely and humanely in relation to ourselves, our fellow humans, other animals . . . nature" and God.[24]

Universal Solidarity

Eco-spirituality understands the cosmos as a network of interdependent beings whose future lies in unstinting collaboration with one another. What concerns one concerns all. Our solidarity is not something we need to create but something already in existence that we need to acknowledge. Universal solidarity is part of God's plan for the new creation.

Self-interest alone, if not appreciation of God's plan, should motivate humans to live in harmony with nature and with one another. Solidarity is the only safe course, given humanity's past record of destroying species after species, and given our present capacity to destroy ourselves by accidental or deliberate nuclear war. Jeremy Rifkin explains how war will become obsolete once we acknowledge our universal solidarity:

> Once we come to see ourselves as part of an indivisible whole, in which every living thing is accountable and indebted to every other living thing for its existence, the very idea of making war will become obsolete. For to make war, within this newly defined context, would be to make war on oneself.[25]

William Sloan Coffin, peace activist and former chaplain at Yale, reached a similar conclusion about the need for global solidarity:

Clearly the only viable future was a global one. Clearly the survival unit in our time was no longer an individual nation or an individual anything; it was the entire human race, plus its environment.[26]

Some people object to talk about universal solidarity if there is any suggestion that nations must yield their sovereignty to a world government.[27] Apart from political scenarios, which can be debated, what is needed on the spiritual level is an expanded consciousness, a planetary consciousness. We need to stretch our consciousness from awareness of our personal or regional problems to include awareness of the planetary ecosystem on which we all depend. "Think globally," as the saying goes.

A new way of thinking, such as we have explored in this chapter, is not enough without a corresponding feeling of kinship and love for our planet. Universal solidarity is fruitless without love. Planetary consciousness realizes in a loving, respectful way the solidarity of all people with the non-human community and with the air, the water, and the earth itself. As Jay McDaniel says:

> . . . we need to learn to feel the presence of other living beings and of the natural world as if they are a part of us. We must feel their presence as if their destinies and our own are intertwined, as if their interests and our own are identified. Stated in biblical terms, we must learn to love our neighbors as ourselves, realizing that our neighbors are part of ourselves.[28]

It was none other than Jesus who said, "You must love your neighbor as yourself" (Mk 12:31). Our neighbors are both human and non-human beings. We are to love them all as God loves them all, in the manner appropriate to each.

There is no genuine love of God that excludes our neighbor. Respectful love for our neighbors makes us willing to listen to them, to listen to what the dolphins and all other creatures are saying. Their wordless music blends into a cosmic symphony that gives continual praise to the creator. The more attuned we become to the harmonics of nature, the more we grow in reverence for the works of God. In the following chapter we will dwell at length on the attitude of reverence.

CHAPTER FIVE

❦

Living Reverently in the New Creation

The two foundational principles of eco-spirituality are interdependence, as described in the previous chapter, and reverence. A growing appreciation of the interdependence of all beings results in an attitude of reverence toward all. If I depend to a greater or lesser extent on others for my welfare, then I must respect them as I respect myself. I cannot come to fulfillment without them. Therefore I cannot treat them with disregard or disrespect. They command my reverence.

Eco-spirituality is obliged to move against the current of irreverence in contemporary society. A society that allows littering along its highways, in its public buildings, on its beaches, in its parks and forests, is irreverent toward the earth. A society that tolerates abortion and euthanasia has lost its reverence toward human life. A society that worships on Sunday but inflicts injustices the rest of the week is irreverent toward God.

The hectic pace which most people maintain in our post-industrial culture is inimical to a spirit of reverence. Reverence is not born in haste but in moments of quiet wonder and appreciation. Hasty living has no time to pause, no time to ponder the beautiful. Haste is blind to everything except the deadline it is rushing to meet; whatever gets in its way is likely to be run over without regret. Haste is intrinsically irreverent. Because of our hyperactive style of life we seldom reverence the simple experience of being alive in a wondrous world. We skim the surface of life rather than experience it in all its richness and depth.

Happily, there are some exceptions to the global proliferation of irreverence. In recent memory the figure of Dr. Albert Schweitzer (1875–1965) stands out as a tireless exponent of reverence for life. Schweitzer developed the ethics of reverence for life at his jungle hospital in the Republic of Gabon, Africa. There, for more than fifty years, he practiced what he preached, demonstrating that reverence is not only feasible but also deeply humanizing.

ALBERT SCHWEITZER

Reverence for life, according to Schweitzer, is based in the first place on an existential realization of one's own living being, the fact that one is alive and wishes to go on living. We realize, further, that we share life with a multitude of other beings who, like us, wish to go on living. We are to reverence the will to live that others have, just as we reverence our own will to live, our own actual life. Reverence for life, says Schweitzer, is a matter of "becoming ruled more and more by the longing to preserve and promote life, and becoming more and more obstinate in resistance to the necessity for destroying or injuring life."[1]

Albert Schweitzer yielded to his longing to advance life when at age thirty he gave up a career in biblical scholarship and music in order to devote himself to healing the most neglected human beings he could find. In Gabon, as he was treating innumerable cases of leprosy and dysentery, Schweitzer tried to enhance the self-respect and self-reliance of his patients by teaching them the basics of agriculture, nutrition, hygiene, and literacy. Sometimes he was in the position of trying to save their lives while they worked against his efforts to help them. He always respected the dignity of their personhood, although he was often exasperated by their ignorance and human failings.

By showing constant reverence for particular individuals in a remote corner of the world, Albert Schweitzer practiced universal reverence. A woman who visited Schweitzer on his birthday every year says:

> I will always feel that the old dying leper woman, whose hands he held all night long, was really I and all the people in the world, the baby he picked up was all the babies in the world, and the ants he protected were really all the animals in the world.[2]

Schweitzer, the humanitarian who reverenced all humanity, was also a lover of non-human creatures. One of his biographers says: "He truly did love creatures simply for being alive, and refused to endanger anything, ants, mosquitoes, rats included, which did him and his hospital no obvious harm."[3] Schweitzer had a fondness for ants, based on the notion that they are beneficial scavengers. Once when his African laborers were driving piles for a new building, Schweitzer instructed them to remove an anthill that stood directly in the way (we are not told how this was accomplished). Similarly, he preferred to put a mosquito out of the room rather than to kill it.

However, Schweitzer could not tolerate termites because they threatened to eat the hardwood pilings that supported his buildings. Termites he exterminated with a newly discovered insecticide, DDT. In Schweitzer's reverence for life, there was a hierarchy of values. Human life had priority.

Creatures actually harmful to human life and or to the hospital were killed unless there was another way of removing the threat.

In taking life, whether large or small, animal or vegetable, Schweitzer accepted personal responsibility. He was willing to pay the price of taking life to preserve other life, but he did not make such decisions lightly. "For Schweitzer even the cutting of a flower or the lopping of a tree were matters for responsible consideration."[4]

Schweitzer developed in himself an almost uncanny degree of empathy for other beings. For example, he could imagine what it must be like to view the world from the eyes of a pelican and was able to write the life of a pelican, in the first person. By reverent compassion he could experience other life in his own life. He was lovingly alert to life as such. Albert Schweitzer was not always totally successful in maintaining the attitude of reverence, for he was only human, but he did his best to enhance life in every way and bring it to its maximum development.

Universal Reverence

We have seen in the example of Albert Schweitzer how it is possible to be penetrated by a sense of the immense value of life, so that one will respect life's every manifestation. Reverence is precisely this attitude of profound, respectful honoring. Reverence stands in frank appreciation or admiration before a reality—such as life—that is awesomely greater than ourselves. Reverence is our proper response to what is sacred.

Eco-spirituality promotes a universal reverence because the sacred is everywhere. As we saw in Chapter 2, the created universe is a holy, God-filled place. There are physical and moral evils in the world, but the world as created by God is radically good, abounding in beauty, ordered from within toward life and growth, ordered toward harmony and healing, ordered toward God. A document issued in 1989 by twenty-four physicists and astronomers calls for reverence toward all creation:

> As scientists, many of us have had profound experiences of awe and reverence before the universe. We understand that what is regarded as sacred is more likely to be treated with care and respect. Our planetary home should be so regarded. Efforts to safeguard and cherish the environment need to be infused with a vision of the sacred.[5]

Reverence issues in a sense of wonder and amazement that expands our awareness. In meditation and contemplative prayer, we are lost in wonder at the mystery of God. The psalmist cries to God: "I thank you for the wonder of my being, for the wonders of all your creation" (Ps 139:14). Some can lose themselves in wonder before the mystery of the littlest living thing. Others are gripped by reverent wonder at the beauty of non-living things such as a magnificent landscape. Albert Schweitzer writes of his fascination with a glass of water catching the rays of the sun:

> If during a meal I catch sight of the light broken up in a glass jug of water into the colours of the spectrum, I can at once become oblivious of everything around me, and unable to withdraw my gaze from the spectacle.[6]

A physicist likewise can be caught up in amazement in the midst of a meticulous search for the ultimate structure of matter:

The physicist approaches his subject with something
near to reverence, compelled by the belief in the mathematical beauty and simplicity of nature, and convinced
that by digging deeper into the bowels of matter, unity
will emerge.[7]

The reverence that the contemplative feels in the presence of God and the reverence that the physicist feels in the
presence of nature are subjectively similar experiences and
perfectly compatible with each other. This is not to say that
God and nature are identical or deserve equal reverence.
Reverence for nature is not irreverence for God; reverence
for nature does not diminish our reverence toward God. God
need not compete with nature for our reverence. Rather, we
can reverence God by reverencing nature, because, as we
have seen in Chapter 2, all creation is permeated with God's
presence.

Eco-spirituality recalls that love for God with all our
heart, soul, mind, and strength is inseparable from love of
our neighbor (Lk 10:27). We understand that showing love
and reverence for our neighbor is a way of showing love and
reverence for God, indeed the primary way.[8] There is no
competition between God and our neighbor, because what
we do to every neighbor we do to God (see Mt 25:40). Reverence for the non-human and non-living things of creation is
an extension of the loving reverence we are to show to every
neighbor.

REVERENCING LIFE

What is life? The phenomenon of life remains mysterious, but we observe that on the biological level all living
systems, even the simplest, show some degree of self-

organization and self-regulation, some control over their boundaries and activities. Beyond this biological life, but based on it, and united with it, is the capacity for spiritual life which belongs to every human person made in the image and likeness of God (see Gen 1:27). "Image and likeness" means precisely this human capacity to participate to some degree in God's own life of knowing and loving, a life of freedom and bliss.

All life is worthy of reverence because it has its ultimate origin in the boundless vitality of the living God. "In you is the source of life," says the psalmist (Ps 36:10). Eco-spirituality is unabashedly pro-life, yet this perspective must be qualified.

Although biological life is the foundation of all other goods, it is not an absolute good which must be preferred to everything else. Nor is the multiplication and preservation of life an absolute good. Biological life is worthy of reverence, but it may be sacrificed for the sake of spiritual life or spiritual values because these are higher than merely biological values. For example, many have preferred to die rather than live without freedom. Some, fewer in number, have given their lives out of sacrificial love so that others might live. Jesus assures us, "No one can have greater love than to lay down his life for his friends" (Jn 15:13). In some circumstances, reverence for one's own or another's life may mean letting go of it by allowing a fatal pathology to run its course without attempting extraordinary countermeasures.

Life is a relative good; death is not always an evil. Lower forms of life must die so that higher forms of life may exist. Even when it comes to human life, the duty to reverence life by preserving it has its limits. As one ethicist puts it: "The Catholic tradition holds that there are values more important than life in the living of life. So, it also holds that there are values more important than life in dying."[9] Such values would include the advancement of one's spiritual life by practicing love for God and neighbor.

Nonetheless, all life deserves to be reverenced and cherished. In the first place we must reverence the dignity and uniqueness of our own humanity. What this means, says Albert Schweitzer, is that we must live in the truth and be faithful to our own deepest calling. "Reverence for one's own life should compel one, whatever the circumstances may be, to avoid all dissimulation and, in general, to become oneself in the deepest and noblest sense."[10]

Reverence for nature will come when humans have recovered the grateful respect for themselves that the psalmist expresses: "I thank you for the wonder of my being, for the wonders of all your creation" (Ps 139:14). A human person transcends all non-human creation by reason of his or her capacity for self-reflection, creative thinking, free choice, language, and altruistic love. The biological basis of this transcendent behavior is the amazing human brain with its billions of nerve cells, each one in direct, orderly communication with more than five thousand other nerve cells in a network as complex and vast as the stars in the universe. Much of this potential goes unused, but our own human potentiality is always to be respected.

Further, we are called to reverence those who share the gift of life with us in the human community and also in the larger community of all carbon-based life forms. On a planet where eighty percent of the people go hungry, and where pollutants in the air and water threaten both human and non-human life, reverence obliges us to be concerned about quality of life for everyone. Quality of life needs to be considered also in dealing with animals. When animals must be used for medical testing and laboratory experimentation, or even in animal farms, reverence obliges us to treat them as gently and humanely as possible.

Difficult questions of balance arise when industrial, residential, or recreational developments expand into wilderness areas. Where does reverence lie when people depend for their survival on hunting endangered species, on cutting for firewood the trees that keep back the encroaching desert, or on clearing rain forests for subsistence agriculture?

Even more difficult questions are raised by genetic engineering. When it comes to crossing and mixing species, and especially when it comes to human genetic engineering, the need for reverence is paramount. Human life is more than a chemical code in the DNA molecule; human life is also the image of divine life, and therefore spiritual and sacred. Reverence for life would be reluctant to tamper with the human gene pool.

REVERENCING EARTH

I remember the first time I visited the Grand Canyon in Arizona. I had seen pictures of it, but these were no preparation for the overpowering experience of being there, walking slowly toward the unfenced rim, seeing the solid earth end in a sudden void almost a mile deep and ten miles across, stretching further than I could see to right and left. After an involuntary gasp at the vastness of the canyon, I was struck by the stillness of the whole panorama. No one in our group of four had much to say because as soon as we spoke, it seemed as if our words were swallowed up by the enormous chasm before us. The proper response was not words but silence. I felt dumb and dwarfed in the presence of something so immense, so primordial. I felt the same reverence I feel in a sacred place at a sacred moment. The Grand Canyon evokes that sort of reverence. It is a place of tremendous majesty. To throw beer cans over the rim, as some do, seems like a desecration.

The reverence that people spontaneously feel at places like the Grand Canyon is the attitude we need to cultivate toward the entire earth. Eco-spirituality honors the earth. We walk the earth with humility and reverence, not with the arrogant air of an insensitive landlord. We do not worship the earth as divine, but respect it as a revelation of the creator; to reverence the earth is to respect the artistry of the divine artist.

Every feature of the global landscape has its value even though we may not be able to identify that value or explain its role in the total ecosystem. It took millions of years for the forces of nature to carve out the Grand Canyon, and every feature of the earth's surface is the result of similar historical processes. The antiquity and functional success of these planetary systems demand reverence.

Our physical environment forms us in obvious as well as subtle ways. We are shaped by the landscape and imbued with the spirit of the place where we live. It could be said that the earth gives birth to us because it conditions the way we live and support ourselves. People in the tropics are different in many ways from people in the arctic; the environment affects their quality of life and also their outlook on life.

It is because the earth shapes and nurtures us that the earth is our mother. People rightly associate the earth with maternal qualities of fruitfulness, growth, creativity, protection, healing, guidance, beneficence. Mother earth deserves a loving reverence similar to that which we show to our human mothers.

During the centuries before Europeans colonized the Americas, native Americans developed an intimate, harmonious relationship with mother earth. In the present state of Maine lived the Wabanakis Nation. One of their chiefs, Big Thunder, wrote:

The Great Spirit is our father, but the earth is our mother. She nourishes us; that which we put into the ground she returns to us, and healing plants she gives us likewise. If we are wounded we go to our mother and seek to lay the wounded part against her, to be healed.[11]

The Sokulk tribe of Nez Perce Indians in eastern Washington refused to mine or plow the earth, or even to cut the tall grass, because the earth was their mother. Their religious leader, Smohalla, says:

You ask me to plow the ground. Shall I take a knife and tear my mother's breast? Then when I die she will not take me to her bosom to rest.

You ask me to dig for stone. Shall I dig under her skin for her bones? Then when I die I cannot enter her body to be born again.

You ask me to cut grass and make hay and sell it and be rich like white men. But how dare I cut off my mother's hair?[12]

More than a century later, at the 1989 hearings conducted by the U.S. Department of Energy, native Americans were still talking about earth as a living organism, a mother. The DOE proposal was to store low grade radioactive waste in salt beds 2,150 feet underground near Carlsbad in southeastern New Mexico. Rex Taloosi, vice president of the 550 member Havasupai tribe of the Grand Canyon, said that Indians believe the earth is "a living organism, and that storing waste inside the earth is like poisoning a human being." He added, "We feel that people should be aware of the sacredness of our Mother Earth and also life upon our Mother Earth."[13]

The Hopi Indians of the southwest perform some of their religious ceremonies in a kiva, which is a mounded structure built over a pit in the ground. The womb-like kiva is a symbol of mother earth from whose flesh all are born. When a coal company began strip-mining operations on land leased to them, the Hopis objected in a vigorous letter to President Richard Nixon:

> The white man, through his insensitivity to the way of nature, has desecrated the face of Mother Earth. The white man's advanced technological capacity has occurred as a result of his lack of regard for the spiritual path and for the way of all living things. The white man's desire for material possessions and power has blinded him to the pain he has caused Mother Earth by his quest for what he calls natural resources.[14]

These native Americans prefer to follow the spiritual path of harmony with mother earth. They regulate their lives according to the pattern that is visible in the annual cycle of planting, growing, harvesting, and resting. In this way they show their reverence for the motherly care of the earth. They walk in step with earth's own rhythms which are like the movement of the creator through the garden of creation (Gen 3:8). Interacting constructively and reverently with their environment, these native Americans have tried not to struggle against the flow of the current but to let it guide them toward the fulfillment that is possible for them in the total community of creation.[15]

REVERENCING THE WORK OF HUMAN HANDS

Most people today live in the artificial environment of a large or small city, not in rural areas. Is it possible to live reverently in the midst of skyscrapers and noisy traffic? Eco-spirituality tries to address the situation in which people actually live and work, the concrete situation. How can we sacralize daily life in the concrete jungle of a modern city?

One approach claims that the sacred is already to be found in the city. It is no longer the thunderstorm that incites feelings of reverence but the thunder of heavy construction or of jet planes taking off. People feel their littleness in front of Mack trucks rather than shaggy buffaloes. In the city we reverence the power of money and the beauty of elegant architecture. Most of all we reverence science and technology. Without remembering that technological progress is a gift from God, we tend to revere the entity that provides our basic needs and keeps us entertained. Carrying this tendency to its extreme, Jacques Ellul says, "Technology is the god who saves. It is good in its essence."[16]

Reverence for technical wizardry is reverence indeed, but less ennobling than Albert Schweitzer's reverence for life or the Hopi Indians' reverence for mother earth. The human penchant for idolatry inclines us to honor the work of our own hands rather than works that come more directly from the hand of God. For lack of a better object of reverence, people prostrate before the ersatz altar of technology, but technology is meant to be humanity's servant, not its master.

Another approach, more fruitful, is to import elements of nature into the city in order to provide something more worthy of reverence. The harshness of the city can be somewhat softened by the presence of green plants and trees, even by a planter box of flowers in the window of an apartment instead of an air conditioner. Shopping malls have occasional oases of greenery. City parks provide places where nature is easily accessible to the urban population. The city of Mobile, Alabama, rather than remove their trees, wisely constructed office and residential buildings around their giant live oaks garlanded with hanging moss.

Another successful approach is to design city buildings and even whole cities in harmony with the environment. Instead of a proliferation of tasteless concrete monstrosities, there will be structures that are functional, intimate, and integral with the land. An editorial in a Hong Kong newspaper laments the passing of "a charm and graciousness that used to lift human hearts in many of the cities of the world."[17] Cities ought to have a charm of their own, commanding appreciation and respect for the products of human ingenuity. In the high desert north of Phoenix, Arizona, a small city designed by Paulo Soleri and built by volunteer labor is slowly rising in the barren hills. Called Arcosanti, the city utilizes solar energy to the maximum and aims at being almost self-sustaining. Soleri is moving toward architecture that is symbiotic with its surroundings.

There is a growing number of architects who are sensitive to the need for harmony with the natural environment. "Their buildings participate with the heat and light of the sun, the cycles of the seasons, the geography of the land and the currents and tides of the winds and water."[18] One example is the American architect Frank Lloyd Wright (1860–1959). The house he designed at Falling Water, Pennsylvania, is built around a large boulder whose upper surface forms the fireplace hearth. A fast-moving stream flows beneath one wing of the building. Because the house seems to grow out of the ground itself, it is difficult to tell where nature ends and human workmanship begins. The house was designed reverently, and it compels our reverence.

Eco-spirituality shows proper respect for the products of human labor. Perhaps this respect is nowhere more appropriate than when it is given to the bread and wine that are consecrated to become the body and blood of Christ in the eucharist. Reverence for the elements of the eucharist, which is "the sacramental center of the New Creation," makes us more alive to the sacredness of all things.[19] Bread is both a gift of mother earth and a product of human labor; wine is "fruit of the vine and work of human hands," as the prayer puts it. If these fabricated materials are worthy of becoming a sacrament that contains the mystery of Christ, then every honest, noble artifact, every honorable expression of human creativity, deserves to be valued and reverenced. Thus, for example, the sixth-century *Rule of St. Benedict* introduces an attitude of reverence when it instructs the cellarer to "regard all utensils and goods of the monastery as sacred vessels of the altar."[20]

THE PATH OF UNIVERSAL REVERENCE

The new creation is here already—though not yet fully —because of the incarnation, passion, and resurrection of Christ. In this context our attitude of universal reverence is a distant echo of God's gaze upon the first creation and God's judgment that it was all "very good" (Gen 1:31). An unnamed Russian pilgrim of the nineteenth century describes how he walked the path of reverence in communion with all creation:

> When I began to pray with the heart, everything around me became transformed and I saw it in a new and delightful way. The trees, the grass, the earth, the air, the light, and everything seemed to be saying to me that it exists to witness to God's love and that it prays and sings of God's glory.[21]

The path of reverence leads to a sense of kinship with other beings and even to a spontaneous love for them as fellow creatures of God. Russian literary tradition furnishes

another example, this time from Starets Zossima in Dostoeyevsky's *The Brothers Karamazov*. Zossima preaches universal respectful love:

> Love all God's creation, the whole and every grain of
> sand in it. Love every leaf, every ray of God's light. Love
> the plants, love everything. If you love everything, you
> will perceive the divine mystery in things. Once you per-
> ceive it, you will begin to comprehend it better every
> day. And you will come at last to love the whole world
> with an all-embracing love.[22]

It might be objected that Zossima's all-embracing love
only sugarcoats the evil that is so evident in the world. The
new creation is threatened by the forces of ecological chaos,
unfortunately assisted by human carelessness. Nature itself
is rife with violence; the law of the jungle often prevails
outside the jungle as well. Death and destruction are ram-
pant from the cellular level to the supernovas exploding in
outer space. The universe came to birth in the violence of the
Big Bang and may come to an equally violent end in the Big
Crunch. Nature is not always benign.

Still, the violence of nature can be seen against a larger
context, an overarching divine plan which can be reverenced
even if it cannot fully be understood. Do we realize that
without death there is no new life? The ancient psalmist
knew that when "the young lions roar for their prey," God
hears their cry and provides them with a gazelle for food (Ps
104:21). The killing is necessary and not deliberately cruel.
Death is willed by God as part of the rhythm of nature. God
is present not only in life but also in death; God transcends
both life and death.

When the Pueblo Indians hunt deer, they do so with an
attitude of humble compassion for the animal that must die.

They sing a song to the deer, asking it to sacrifice itself that the Indians might live. Lying in wait along a deer trail, they kill the first animal that offers itself to them. Afterward there is a prayer to the slaughtered deer imploring its pardon, explaining the need for food, and instructing it to give a favorable report to the other deer spirits.[23] Before the meat is eaten, permission is requested from the animal's spirit; the meal becomes a sacrament of communion with the great web of life in which all are entwined. The Hopi and Totonac Indians ask permission from any tree or living plant that they cut for use in their religious ceremonies.[24] Thus life is reverenced even in the taking of life.

The path of universal reverence is not the path of sentimentality or naiveté. We know there is a difference between killing for food or protection, and killing for sport or for luxury-garments. Where there is unnecessary violence or cruelty, eco-spirituality strives to put reverence. Reverence would try to reduce the violence involved in the gradual poisoning of the soil and water with chemical waste. Reverence would also try to counteract the chronic social violence that prevents two-thirds of the world's population from fulfilling basic needs and aspirations while the remaining one-third consumes eighty percent of the world's resources.

Reverence honors God by actively honoring God's creation. In addition to passive appreciation, there is need for creative engagement with the world. Reverence is as reverence does. If there is merely a feeling of respect but no effort to act respectfully, it is not reverence. True reverence passes beyond mere admiration, beyond mere contemplation, to take appropriate action. Reverence leads to personal commitment and practical service.

There are situations, it is true, when the most beneficial behavior toward the environment, or toward a species or individual, is simply to let it be. Nature is self-regulating, and human interference may only make matters worse. In these cases, reverence is shown in watchful concern, not in intervention. More frequently, though, reverence involves a positive commitment to the well-being of all things by fostering, protecting, restoring, assisting, and developing them. Reverence is practical and constructive.

Reverence for all things is the essential attitude of a caretaker who wisely and gently enhances the quality of life wherever possible. The role of humankind in God's creation is to be the faithful, prudent caretaker who walks the path of universal reverence. Each created entity has its own ordered structure, its own purpose and mysterious destiny. To live reverently in the new creation is to respect and celebrate the integrity of all that is.

CHAPTER SIX

❧

Global Healing and Reconciliation

By his incarnation, death and resurrection, Christ has inaugurated the renewal of all creation, both human and non-human. "He is Lord of all" (Acts 10:36). The new creation is creation redeemed, creation reconciled. Christians are called to be co-workers in Christ's work of universal renewal. The task before us at the end of this millennium is daunting, "for the whole creation is waiting with eagerness" to be freed from its slavery to corruption (Rom 8:19).

Within this perspective, eco-spirituality asks what can be done to foster the healing, reconciling process taking place in each individual heart and in all creation. In this chapter we consider some of the things that need to be done on the global level, by cooperative endeavors. The following chapter will explore things that can be done locally through individual initiatives.

THE GLOBAL CRISIS

"The whole creation," said St. Paul in the first century, "has been groaning in labor pains" (Rom 8:22). Two millennia later, the new creation still has not come fully to birth. The groans of mother earth go on increasing in intensity as

99

humanity multiplies the pressures on major terrestrial systems—the atmosphere, the soil, the water.

Each year millions of tons of garbage, toxic chemicals, medical wastes, fertilizers, and crude oil are dumped, accidentally or deliberately, into the oceans. Urban air pollution, due especially to automobiles and industrial emissions, insidiously undermines human health, corrodes historical monuments, poisons lakes and streams, kills trees and crops.

A severely degraded environment blights the quality of life for future generations. The long-term hazards were noted by a United Methodist missionary, Howard Heiner, who participated in a Church World Service project in Latin American during 1987–1988. He saw extensive areas which once were fertile and now are desolate:

> One can stand in the Andes and the valleys and see sheet erosion. Just the whole valley, tremendous destruction. That, quite frankly, challenges my faith. The misery and the death which this portends to me for the generations to come is frightening. . . . Humankind must face the fact that we are destroying the earth.[1]

If not actually destroying the earth, we are critically wounding it and rendering large areas unproductive. At the same time, the demand for food and raw materials is rising because of population growth and the desire of the poor for their legitimate share of the fruits of the earth. For the short term, economies continue to grow, drawing on reserves of non-renewable resources and not counting all the environmental expenses. In the long term, there are limits to growth, and planetary costs that will have to be paid. If our generation refuses to be accountable, those who come after us will have to pay the price.

Among our more notable bequests to future generations

will be the rising piles of refuse from our throwaway culture. Because the volume of garbage goes on increasing, and available landfill sites are nearing their capacity, waste disposal has become a bothersome and expensive problem. Still more problematic are the hazardous wastes, especially if radioactive. The plutonium from nuclear power plants and the production of weapons remains lethal for 500,000 years.

While everyone agrees that something should be done about all the refuse, people do not care to have the solution located in their back yard, particularly in the case of hazardous wastes. In 1987 a barge bearing three thousand tons of ordinary garbage from New York City was unable to find a place to dump its cargo. Six states and three foreign countries refused to take it. Eight weeks later the barge, named Mobro, returned to New York where its load was eventually burned and buried. Perhaps one lesson is that waste is best controlled or disposed of where it is produced.

According to Marian Chertow, president of the Solid Waste Agency in Connecticut, the solid waste problem is manageable in principle, at least for non-hazardous wastes. Countries such as Switzerland and Japan are far advanced in disposal methods. Recommended is an integrated approach consisting of four practices.

First, to produce less trash. For example, by paring excess packaging, and by cleaning and reusing things.

Second, to recycle trash or turn garbage into compost. There are ways to produce ethanol fuel from organic waste biomass, for example.

Third, to burn non-recyclables in waste-to-energy plants, using the heat to generate electricity.

Fourth, to dump the unusable remainder into landfills. At present, Americans send eighty percent of their garbage to the landfill, as the primary rather than the ultimate method of disposal.[2]

We have been conditioned to buy and use disposable goods, and then pitch them or flush them and forget them forever. At the same time we have learned to increase our level of tolerance for a polluted environment. As Thomas Berry puts it, all the ingenuity of advertising and technology is aimed at "moving the greatest volume of natural resources through the consumer economy at the greatest possible speed to the waste heap."[3]

To change these habits will not be easy. We have even littered outer space, a thousand miles from earth, with thousands of tons of debris. Pollution will not be brought under control without a revolution in social attitudes and behavior. This revolution, if it comes about, will lead us away from excessive production and consumption, and toward a way of living that is durable or sustainable far into the future.

Post-industrial societies have aimed at a steady increase of profits, regardless of environmental degradation, but this rate of economic growth cannot continue indefinitely on a planet with finite resources. Unless there is a change, "we will simply continue to add fuel to our own funeral pyre."[4]

WHO IS TO BLAME?

When we begin to comprehend the dimensions of our ecological crisis and to picture the spiritual revolution needed to change our present course, there is a tendency to look for a scapegoat. Who or what is responsible for getting us into this mess? If the responsibility can be laid at the feet of others, then they can be held accountable for repairing the damages, and the rest of us are absolved of responsibility.

Periodically the finger of blame is pointed at big business, at the government with its wasteful ways, or even at Christianity. Christianity is accused of downplaying the goodness of the material world in order to direct our aspirations toward a better world in heaven. Or Christian theology is accused of granting a license to dominate and exploit creation instead of tending it as a loving caretaker.

In fact, if blame must be handed out, there is enough to go around for everyone. Each individual is responsible for his or her own choices which either add to the ecological crisis or help relieve it. As a way of building a sustainable society, tactics of accusation and denunciation are counterproductive. What is needed is a sweeping change of attitude and practice. What is needed is the cooperation of all parties in the interests of saving the earth.

Solutions are available for many of our ecological problems, but they depend on spirituality as much as on technology. For there is a correlation between abuse of the earth and abuse of persons. Both spring from the same attitude of irreverence. When we cease to exploit other people, especially the powerless, then we may cease to exploit the earth. As theologian Sean McDonagh puts it: "The stance men and women take towards the earth is of a piece with their stance towards their fellow human beings."[5]

CONSUMER SOCIETY

Eco-spirituality does not underestimate the magnitude of the spiritual conversion demanded. What is needed is nothing less than an axial shift from scientific materialism to Christian love and justice. As one observer puts it, "We must move from a society oriented to satisfy the artificial wants of a few to one committed to satisfy the basic needs of all."[6] Justice, in contrast to selfishness, would permit all people to satisfy their basic needs and develop their highest potential. Justice is universally life-enhancing.

Most people do not set out to ruin this planet deliberately and maliciously. Nevertheless, a self-interested, consumerist style of life eventually leads to such a fate. Out of self-interest, most nations and most individuals tend to choose the advantages of materialism as a sure path to human fulfillment, regardless of the consequences. The Worldwatch Institute accepts this propensity as virtually inevitable:

> Societies across the ideological spectrum have persisted in equating quality of life with increased consumption. Personal self-worth typically is measured by possessions, just as social progress is judged by GNP growth.[7]

Pope John Paul II uses the term "superdevelopment" to describe the condition of consumer societies, especially in contrast to the numerous underdeveloped countries in the world. In his encyclical *On Social Concerns*, he says trenchantly:

> This superdevelopment, which consists in an excessive availability of every kind of material goods for the benefit of certain social groups, easily makes people slaves of "possession" and of immediate gratification, with no other horizon than the multiplication or continual replacement of the things already owned with others still better. This is the so-called civilization of "consumption" or "consumerism," which involves so much "throwing away" and "waste."[8]

In this encyclical, the pope acknowledges the "structures of sin" (n. 36) that affect conditions of life in superdeveloped societies. Underlying these sinful social structures, which are responsible for much of the environmental degradation and which can be changed only with difficulty, are the sinful attitudes of individual human hearts and minds. These attitudes of greed, gluttony, selfishness, fear, and arrogance are the deeper causes of superdevelopment. In the words of one theologian of ethics, "Sin is the ultimate polluter of the world."[9] In the words of St. Paul, "Greed is the same thing as worshiping a false god" (Col 3:5).

These sinful attitudes can be changed, by the grace of God, through a process of religious conversion. The roots of our ecological crisis are ethical and spiritual; the corrective should be sought on the same level. Before and beyond the task of restoring nature, there is the task of healing human hearts and reconciling human minds that are narrow and closed. If our minds and hearts are fully open to nature, neighbor, and God, there can be a gradual global transformation comparable to a new creation. Eco-spirituality believes that spiritual healing will lead to ecological healing.

APPROACHES TO HEALING

Like a religion or like a political ideology, the modern ecological movement contains a potentiality for healing and reconciling but also a potentiality for causing controversy. Some people embrace ecology as if it were a religion in itself. For example, in Leningrad, USSR, a grassroots environmental effort is confronting some of the water pollution problems associated with nearby Lake Ladoga. One of the movement's leaders, geologist Sergei Tsvetkov, explained his idea of ecology as a religious phenomenon:

> Ecology to me is the contemporary religion. It's only on the basis of ecology that spiritual integration of the

whole global community is possible. Simple love for nature must enter into the consciousness of each living human being. We have been at war with nature for centuries. We human beings think that we are the czars of
nature. We just usurped this role—we were not
given it.[10]

Ecologically concerned persons from traditional Christian backgrounds usually attempt to situate their environmental activism within their Christian theology and spirituality rather than to embrace ecology as a new religion. For
centuries the dominant forms of Christian theology and spirituality have been redemption-centered. Partly as a reaction
to this preponderant emphasis, and partly as an attempt to
find a basis with broader ecumenical appeal, many ecological Christians are turning to a creation-centered spirituality.

A third alternative, Christian eco-spirituality, attempts
to integrate redemption-centered and creation-centered
spiritualities by focusing on the new creation inaugurated by
Christ in his redemptive incarnation, passion, and resurrection. The following sections explain these alternatives.

Redemption-Centered

On account of the original sin of the first human beings,
God cursed the ground so that it would yield thorns and
thistles, and would produce edible plants only by the sweat
of the human brow (see Gen 3:17–19). There was no way
that human beings could extricate themselves from God's
punishment. Instead, their situation continued to deterio-
rate, and the earth shared in the universal misery:

Ravaged, ravaged the earth will be, despoiled, despoiled, for Yahweh has uttered this word. The earth is

mourning, pining away, the pick of earth's people are withering away. The earth is defiled by the feet of its inhabitants, for they have transgressed the laws, violated the decree, broken the everlasting covenant (Is 24:3–5).

This devastation continued until "the kindness and love of God our Savior for mankind were revealed" (Ti 3:4). God sent his Son into a fallen world to share fully in our human nature, "so that by his death he could set aside him who held the power of death, namely the devil, and set free all those who had been held in slavery all their lives by the fear of death" (Heb 2:14). Christ became a compassionate high priest who sacrificed himself on the cross for all, because he alone was "able to expiate the sins of the people" (Heb 2:17).

On the basis of this reading of scripture, redemption-centered theology stresses human participation in Christ's sacrificial atonement, because the effects of original sin continue to afflict the world even though the sin itself may be forgiven through baptism. These effects are felt in resistance to transformation and growth, in opposition to change and conversion. On account of original sin there is disharmony where there should be harmonious interaction.

Redemption-centered spirituality displays a tendency toward dualistic, subject/object thinking which exalts the human apart from the rest of creation. Material, non-human creation is not considered evil, but is not highly valued "because this world as we know it is passing away" (1 Cor 7:31). Healing and reconciliation are perceived primarily on the interpersonal level, while the consequences of Christ's saving work on a wounded cosmos are underplayed.

Holiness as perfect love is achieved—by the help of divine grace—through asceticism, prayer, the practice of virtue, and acceptance of God's will. The three ways of purgation, illumination, and union lead to the kingdom of heaven. Redemption-centered thinking has formed our mainstream theology and spirituality since the fourth century, with exponents like St. Augustine, St. Bernard, St. Anselm, Thomas à Kempis, Cardinal Bossuet, and Adolphe Tanquerey.

Creation-Centered

This tradition—implicit in St. Irenaeus, John Scotus Erigena, Hildegard of Bingen, St. Francis of Assisi, and Meister Eckhart—has been rediscovered and promoted in recent times. Dominican theologian Matthew Fox and his associates at the Institute in Culture and Creation Spirituality at Holy Names College in Oakland, California, are exploring diligently this tradition within the context of individual and group process, art-as-meditation, ritual, and other forms of creative self-expression.

Before the original sin there was the original blessing of all creation by the creator who pronounced it "very good" (Gen 1:31). Creation-centered theology emphasizes the inalienable goodness of the cosmos, without denying the mysterious presence of evil. In keeping with this positive emphasis, the human individual is always seen against the horizon of the whole cosmos and never separate from it or dominant over it. A vital cosmology composed of science, mysticism, and art replaces a mechanistic, Newtonian cosmology. Humans have a responsibility to live as creatures among creatures, in balance with the rest of God's creation. Humans are called to be co-creators with God of a new world, and to thirst after justice for all. As God loves this earth, we are to love our own earthiness. Creation-spirituality pursues holiness by four paths:

1. The affirmation of God's goodness and presence within creation.
2. Dropping ego-projections in order to seek God in contemplative darkness or silent suffering, and in letting be.
3. Rising to new life as we set our creative imagination free for fresh discoveries of God.
4. A compassionate, Spirit-guided struggle against injustice leading to a new, transformed creation.[11]

The overarching symbol of creation-centered spirituality is the cosmic Christ. The cosmic Christ is not so much the historical Jesus or the personal Savior but the mythic figure who inspires "a living cosmology, an awakened creativity and a deeper commitment to compassion."[12] The cosmic Christ is Jesus who does "what he sees the Father doing" (Jn 5:19). The cosmic Christ can be ourselves too, acting in prophetic roles, for Jesus promised: "Whoever believes in me will perform the same works as I do myself, and will perform even greater works" (Jn 14:12). Creation-centered spirituality looks for the cosmic Christ to usher in "a spiritual and cultural renaissance that can heal the most poignant and urgent pain of our time—the crucifixion of Mother Earth."[13]

Eco-Spirituality

As described in this book, eco-spirituality integrates features of redemption-centered spirituality and creation-centered spirituality in a movement toward the final reconciliation of opposites in the new creation. In the new creation, says St. Paul, "There can be neither Jew nor Greek, there can be neither slave nor freeman, there can be neither male nor female—for you are all one in Christ Jesus" (Gal 3:28).

Indeed the process of global healing and reconciliation has already begun, since "God was in Christ reconciling the world to himself" (2 Cor 5:19). In the mystery of Christ, creation has been elevated to a higher dignity and destiny than it enjoyed originally. The opening prayer for the liturgy on Thursday of the fourth week of Easter declares: "Father, in restoring human nature you have given us a greater dignity than we had in the beginning." Yet much still remains to be accomplished through the cooperative, co-creative efforts of all God's people.

The opening chapters of the Bible describe the freshness and integrity of creation springing forth at the divine word, "Let it be." This pristine harmony was not preserved. The Bible itself traces a spiral of continual corruption, and this account is corroborated by everything we know from history and archeology.[14] Ancient cities were well fortified for warfare; ancient temples show signs of ritual human sacrifice. Ancient stone slabs depict mutilated prisoners, and burial grounds sometimes contain evidence of head-hunting and violent death.[15]

The work of reconciliation accomplished by Christ was essential in order to redeem humankind from every form of iniquity. Sin, as noted above, is the root cause of all preventable degradation of God's creation. The Bible sees sin "not merely as moral, but as cosmic disorder."[16] According to the book of Genesis, when God saw how corrupt and depraved the human race had become, God decided to destroy all life on earth by means of a flood (Gen 6:11–13).

Beyond personal reconciliation, Christ's saving work extends to everything on earth, bringing about the new creation foretold in ancient prophecies. "Look, I am doing something new, now it emerges; can you not see it?" (Is 43:19). The cross of Christ in no way sets the Christian against the natural world. By the wood of the cross the natural world is involved in the reconciling effect of Christ's death. The tree of the cross is nature's noblest contribution to the new creation.

Humans hold a pre-eminent but not exclusive place within the new creation. The human community is incomplete without the non-human community of animals and plants, dry land and oceans (see Pss 104, 148). Some biblical promises presuppose the solidarity of humankind with and within nature, all sharing "the same glorious freedom as the children of God" (Rom 8:21). "The wolf and the young lamb will feed together" (Is 65:25).

The new creation, when fully realized, will mean harmony not only within the human sphere but also between human and non-human, spiritual and material, sacred and profane. Such distinctions will not be obliterated but will no longer appear as sharp polarizations. All will have their place as integral parts of the whole, "so that God may be all in all" (1 Cor 15:28). Thus Christian eco-spirituality is holistic and inclusive.

The realization of this harmonic, holistic vision does not come without a struggle against the resistance of the powers of chaos. The agony of Jesus on the cross was the decisive but not the final phase of this struggle. St. Paul compares the struggle to labor pains—creative but nonetheless painful (Rom 8:22).

God's master plan for creation is still working itself out. Creation is to be seen as a continuing, dynamic process guided by incomprehensible love. God's purpose is lovingly to draw all beings into blissful union with the divine being in the new creation. "He would bring everything together under Christ, as head, everything in the heavens and everything on earth" (Eph 1:10). Eco-spirituality trusts God's plan of love to bring the new creation into final integration, but not without our co-creative cooperation in imitation of

Christ's own reconciling work. Both scripture and early patristic tradition are consistent with this view, as the following
section explains.

EARLY TRADITION

Salvation history is the record of God's creative, reconciling love for humanity and for everything else that has
come into being. Nothing is too insignificant to claim the
affection of the creator who knows "all the birds in the sky"
(Ps 50:11), nor too multitudinous to claim the creator's personal care, for "he fixes the number of the stars, he calls each
one by its name" (Ps 147:4). According to the story of Jonah,
God spared the repentant city of Nineveh out of love for its
120,000 inhabitants, "to say nothing of all the animals" (Jon
4:11). The cattle and sheep of Nineveh fasted in solidarity
with the human population to atone for the city's wickedness (Jon 3:7).

God's healing love embraces humankind, animals and
plants, the land that was specially promised to the chosen
people, and the whole material cosmos. This immense divine
love became flesh in Jesus Christ: "For this is how God loved
the world: he gave his only Son" (Jn 3:17). The incarnation,
death, and resurrection of Christ have universal redemptive
effects. Christ's redemptive work was creative, and it revealed hidden dimensions of God's original purpose for
creation.

God's plan revolves around the theandric mystery of
Jesus Christ "through whom he made the ages," that is, the
universe, and by whom he sustains all things (Heb 1:1–3).
Not only is Christ at the origin of creation, he is also the goal
toward which everything moves, "the Alpha and the
Omega, who was dead and has come to life again" (Rev 1:9).

Christ is the one through whom all things came to be and through whom all things, in their interdependent complexity, exist (1 Cor 8:6). Christ is also the good shepherd who cares for the flock of beings and gently guides them to their destinies. The good shepherd lays down his life for his flock, then rises again to bring the flock new life, hope, and peace.[17]

The centrality of Christ in God's plan is perhaps nowhere better expressed than in the following text of St. Paul:

> He is the image of the unseen God, the first-born of all creation, for in him were created all things in heaven and on earth: everything visible and everything invisible, thrones, ruling forces, sovereignties, powers—all things were created through him and for him. He exists before all things and in him all things hold together, and he is the head of the body, that is, the church. He is the beginning, the first-born from the dead, so that he should be supreme in every way, because God wanted all fullness to be found in him and through him to reconcile all things to him, everything in heaven and everything on earth, by making peace through his death on the cross (Col 1:15–20).

The risen Christ is here presented as supreme and universal Lord, reconciling and drawing to himself not only humanity but all things in heaven and on earth.

Examples from the patristic period will show that this biblical perspective was maintained and deepened by subsequent Christian reflection. Patristic theologians acknowledged Christ as the Lord of creation. They saw human and cosmic history as a movement toward the ultimate goal of union with God in the new creation.

St. Athanasius (328–373) was the principal defender of

orthodoxy against Arianism in the fourth century. He did not separate God's original work of creation from God's work of re-creation in Christ, but saw them as stages in the realization of a single divine plan. "For Athanasius, there exists an unbroken continuity between creation and redemption, which have been wrought by the same Creator-God whose purpose is the reconciliation of all things in time and eternity."[18]

In one of his discourses to non-Christians, St. Athanasius compares the universe with its carefully balanced components to a mixed choir of men, women, and children, young and old, all singing in harmony. The conductor, who is Christ, directs them all according to his Father's will, so that each part performs its own proper function and all together produce "the beauty and harmony of a single, well-ordered universe."[19]

St. Maximus the Confessor (580–662) was a prolific and profound Byzantine writer who envisioned the human person as a microcosm uniting the extremes of rationality and animality, and bringing them into unity. Christ, the second Adam, is the microcosm par excellence because he unites both the created and the uncreated, bringing all creation into union with God. The role of humanity on earth is actively to assist the savior in drawing all things from antagonism and dividedness into harmony. This goal will be achieved "through the union of all things, attaining God in whom there is no division."[20]

The monastic and mystical tradition is represented by Isaac the Syrian, bishop of Nineveh, who died in the year 700. Love is, according to Isaac, the principal force of healing and reconciliation in a suffering world. Isaac is remarkable for wanting to extend the healing force of love, which he calls "the burning of the heart" not only to fellow humans but also to irrational beings, and even to reptiles. The sight of any suffering creature arouses in him "the force of mercy which moves the heart by great compassion."[21] Commenting on Isaac's compassion for the whole creation, Orthodox theologian Vladimir Lossky says: "In his way to union with God, he in no way leaves creatures aside, but gathers together in his love the whole cosmos disordered by sin, that it may at last be transfigured by grace."[22]

If, according to biblical and patristic thought, Christ is the "last Adam" (1 Cor 15:45), his human mother Mary is the new Eve or even the new Eden. Mary symbolizes the new Eden which is the earth reconciled to God and transfigured by grace. Of Mary, the church sings with the psalmist: "Our earth shall yield its fruit" (Ps 85:13). The fruit of this fertile earth is Christ; it is through Mary that Christ is connected physically to the world of materiality.

Earth is the primordial "mother of all the living," the matrix of all life-forms (Gen 3:20). This mothering, nurturing earth is the land favored by the Lord (Ps 85:2). St. Theodore the Studite (759–826), a Byzantine theologian and abbot of Studios, developed the symbolism of Mary as the favored land:

> It seems to me that the blessed Joel is referring to her when he cries out: "Do not be afraid, O land; be glad and rejoice, for the Lord has done great things for you." For Mary is a land. . . . She is the land, not cursed like the former land whose crops were full of thorns and thistles, but blessed by the Lord. Blessed is the fruit of the womb of this land, as sacred Scripture says![23]

The civilizations of antiquity personified mother earth and sometimes divinized her as Gaia, the daughter of Chaos. Christian tradition proposes instead the figure of Mary, mother of the one who heals all humanity and reconciles

earth with God. In Mary, as the new Eve/Eden, we see a
flawless image of creation redeemed, reconciled, transformed—the new creation.

From Ideal to Real

The inspiring vision depicted by the Bible and patristic
theologians needs to be made concrete. Spiritual ideals have
to find tangible embodiment. The new creation calls for our
cooperation. There is no other way to implement a grand
design than by deliberate effort, patiently putting one foot in
front of the other.

Where do we begin? Fortunately, we do not lack people
who are eager to tell us where to begin. Some of these voices
will speak to us in the present section, especially the voices of
international organizations speaking about ecological responsibility. Eco-spirituality listens for the ethical or religious
message in these statements, knowing that only a radical
change of attitude, a spiritual conversion, can get to the root
of our environmental problems. For example, old-growth
redwoods in California will be in danger until loggers come
to value these giant, living trees more than they value a quick
profit.

Yet, as we promote global healing and reconciliation, we
are also concerned about the jobs and well-being of the loggers, not only about the trees. Issues of ecology and social
justice are interwoven because human beings form an organic whole with their environment. Eco-spirituality sees a
vital linkage between preserving the environment and honoring the rights of all people to enjoy the fruits of the earth
and to live in suitable dignity.[24] Nations of the northern
hemisphere have achieved their high standard of living, at
least in part, by economically enslaving people of other

countries and exploiting their natural resources. There is no new creation, no sustainable future for the planet, if the needs of the poor go unsatisfied.

United Nations

Because environmental degradation is a global problem, the UN is a logical place for working out collaborative solutions. The UN sponsors a permanent council for environmental affairs (UNEP: United Nations Environment Programme), and an emergency environmental aid center. In addition, the UN General Assembly adopted in 1982 a World Charter for Nature offering guidelines and principles for protecting our planetary environment. In the preamble of this charter, the international community notes that "civilization is rooted in nature," and goes on to say that "living in harmony with nature gives man the best opportunities for the development of his creativity, and for rest and recreation." They affirm that "every form of life is unique, warranting respect regardless of its worth to man," and that "the conservation of nature and natural resources contributes to justice and the maintenance of peace."[25]

World Council of Churches

At its Sixth Assembly at Vancouver in 1983, the World Council invited its member churches to focus attention on "justice, peace, and the integrity of all creation." These concerns, abbreviated as JPIC, were understood to be vitally interconnected. In 1990 in Seoul, there was a "World Convocation on Justice, Peace and the Integrity of Creation," attended by four hundred voting representatives. The results of this convocation were on the agenda of the World Council's Seventh Assembly in Canberra, Australia, 1991.

Of the ten Affirmations of Faith accepted at Seoul, the

seventh says, "We affirm the creation as beloved of God,"
and the eighth adds, "We affirm that the earth is the Lord's."
Describing what is meant by integrity of creation, the group
detected two aspects:

> The integrity of creation has a social aspect, which we
> recognize as peace with justice, and an ecological aspect,
> which we recognize in the self-renewing, sustainable
> character of natural ecosystems.[26]

Orthodoxy

In 1987, partly in response to the Sixth General Assembly in Vancouver, there was an Inter-Orthodox Consultation
on Orthodox Perspectives on Creation in Sofi, Bulgaria.
Later, in 1989, a symposium was held on Orthodoxy and the
Ecological Crisis at Ligonier, Pennsylvania. The consensus
statement issued by participants at this symposium lays the
blame for the ecological crisis primarily on human sinful-
ness. They call for a radical change of heart, to be maintained
by prayer, fasting, asceticism, repentance and reception of
the sacraments. For "creation is raised and transfigured as
the individual is raised and transfigured."[27] The redemption
and transfiguration of the earth is humanity's responsibility
in union with Christ. They explain their view theologically:

> The birth of Christ reflects the love of God for the whole
> created order, not just for humanity. Jesus Christ came to
> sacrifice himself in order to raise the whole world. The
> life of Christ exemplifies the love which we are called to
> give in redeeming creation.[28]

In a further development, the Holy Synod of the Ecumenical Patriarchate of Constantinople is establishing a feast
day on September 1 "For the Protection of the Environ-

ment." This date is the first day of the Orthodox ecclesiastical year. "A Greek hymnographer of Holy Mount Athos has been assigned the task of preparing a service for the new feast."[29]

The Vatican

The encyclical *On Social Concerns* issued at the end of 1987 contains Pope John Paul's first, sketchy analysis of the ecological crisis. Quoting the 1967 encyclical *On the Development of Peoples (Populorum Progressio)*, John Paul II considers nature in relation to "the development of the whole person and of every human person."[30] He explains the biblical mandate to exercise dominion over creation: "The dominion granted to man by the Creator is not an absolute power, nor can one speak of a freedom to 'use and misuse' or to dispose of things as one pleases."[31] Under the heading of "ecological concern," the pope notes "a greater realization of the limits of available resources, and the need to respect the integrity and cycles of nature."[32]

On the occasion of the World Day of Peace, January 1, 1990, Pope John Paul II returned to the subject of ecology in a message entitled "Peace with God the Creator, Peace with All of Creation." Here he reflects on the biblical account of creation, observing that if humanity is not at peace with God, "then earth itself cannot be at peace."[33] Thus he maintains that "the ecological crisis is a moral crisis," and that this is particularly evident in the widespread loss of "respect for life, and above all for the dignity of the human person."[34] He calls also for respect for the order and integrity of creation. Referring to Vatican Council II, he states the principle that "the earth is ultimately a common heritage, the fruits of which are for the benefit of all," and affirms the universal "right to a safe environment."[35]

The pope urges cooperation on the international and

interreligious level, as well as an education in ecological responsibility that would lead to a conversion from the consumerist lifestyle. "Simplicity, moderation and discipline, as well as a spirit of sacrifice, must become a part of everyday life, lest all suffer the negative consequences of the careless habits of a few."[36] In conclusion, John Paul evokes the memory of St. Francis of Assisi, patron of those who promote ecology and the classic model of being at peace with God and with all creation.

World Conferences

In 1986 the World Wide Fund for Nature sponsored a conference on religion and nature at Assisi for representatives of the world's five largest religions. Unable to agree on a common statement, each religion offered its own declaration. The Christian declaration claims that human dominion over nature is not a license to abuse but a stewardship "in symbiosis with all creatures."[37] The Jewish declaration affirms "the autonomy of all living creatures as the value which our religious tradition must now teach to all of its believers."[38] For Islam, which means peace and submission, it is only when we submit to the will of God that we can find peace: "Peace within us as individuals, peace between man and man, and peace between man and nature."[39] Buddhism, rooted in compassion, loving kindness, and the pursuit of happiness for all sentient beings, emphasizes respect for life and for the environment "since human beings as well as other non-human sentient beings depend upon the environment as the ultimate source of life and well-being."[40] Finally, the Hindu declaration on nature locates both humanity and divinity within creation, not apart from it: "The divine is not exterior to creation, but expresses itself through natural phenomena."[41] Because humankind is integrally linked to the whole of creation, we are to reverence all animal and plant life. According to an ancient Hindu saying, "The earth is our mother, and we are all her children."

The Fourth Biennial Congress "On the Fate and the Hope of the Earth" met in a third world country, at Managua, Nicaragua in 1989. The congress intended to go to the root of our environmental crises, but did not pursue that root to its ultimate spiritual ground. Still, they offer a searching analysis of the intertwined economic, social, and ecological factors, plus helpful suggestions for efficient international action. The centerpiece of their declaration is "that it is a fundamental human right for all the world's people to live and develop in a healthy environment."[42]

Pastoral Letters

As of 1990, the U.S. Catholic Conference of Bishops has not yet issued a pastoral letter on ecology. In their 1986 letter, *Economic Justice for All*, the bishops take note of the ecological crisis and commit themselves to leave an enhanced natural environment to future generations. They state this principle:

> The resources of the earth have been created by God for the benefit of all, and we who are alive today hold them in trust. This is a challenge to develop a new ecological ethic that will help shape a future that is both just and sustainable.[43]

The bishops of the Philippines were the first to issue a pastoral letter on ecology in early 1988. They describe the original bounty and beauty of their islands, where "intricate pathways bind all the creatures together in a mutually supportive community."[44] All this is being rapidly destroyed because of human thoughtlessness, greed, and the "exploit-

ative mentality." The bishops call environmental degradation "the ultimate pro-life issue." They propose a new vision
with the hope of reestablishing the world on the foundation
of Christ. "The destruction of any part of creation, especially
the extinction of species, defaces the image of Christ which is
etched in creation."

Later in 1989 the Catholic bishops of northern Italy issued their pastoral letter on ecology. Their starting point is
the now accepted principle: "Every human being has the
fundamental right to live in an environment suitable to his
health and well-being."[45] The bishops set forth three basic
criteria for ethical interaction with the environment: respect,
moderation, and attention to the quality of life. "Respect for
the environment," they say, "is a gratitude toward God, and
activities concerned with preserving the beauty of the natural environment are not far from being a form of praise and
worship."[46] Moderation in consumption allows sharing with
the poor, and permits future generations to have a base for
development. Under "quality of life," the bishops expand
their concern from the purely natural environment to the
living conditions of people, especially in highly polluted
cities.

Planning Globally

In this chapter we have reflected on numerous approaches to healing our wounded world. Reconciliation of
humanity with nature is the extension or accompaniment of
the effort to reconcile humans with one another and with
God. By listening to God's word and doing God's will, we
move toward reconciliation with God, and at the same time
move toward total global healing in the new creation.

Listening is itself a healing and reconciling practice, because it relaxes our closed and biased mind in an attitude of openness. As we listen more intently, we begin to hear, with St. Paul, the groaning of creation in its "slavery to corruption" (Rom 8:21), and the feeling of compassion grows in our heart. "There is no other way to restore a broken relationship," says Jane Blewett of the Earth Community Center, Laurel, Maryland, "no other way to mend the rift that has separated people from the earth."[47]

After listening and after a conversion of attitude comes the time for action. This chapter has suggested some possibilities for cooperation with others to reverse the process of global environmental destruction. These efforts will not always be welcomed or successful. Where we might expect to find helpful collaboration, we will sometimes find deliberate obstruction. Eco-spirituality is prepared for a lengthy struggle before all creation is "brought into the same glorious freedom as the children of God" (Rom 8:21).

However, if one is blocked at the global level, perhaps one can still move on the personal level of one's own life. The following chapter discusses a program of action on the individual level. While eco-spirituality thinks globally, it is ready to act on a much smaller scale for the sake of contributing in whatever way to the global transformation.

CHAPTER SEVEN

❦

Eco-Spiritual Living

Our temptation, in the face of overwhelming ecological problems, is to give in to a feeling of helplessness. What can any individual do to solve a global crisis? The answer is, "Not much, but individual efforts soon add up." One person's effort to car-pool or use public transportation may be negligible, but if thousands of people were to make the same effort, the difference would be apparent to all. The negative effect on the quality of the atmosphere of one internal-combustion engine on the highway is negligible, but thousands of those engines traveling millions of miles are causing critical levels of air pollution.

On the outskirts of a city in the northwestern United States, one family resolved to disconnect their house from the public utility and to provide their own electricity from solar energy. This decision entailed an initial investment in solar panels, storage batteries, and twelve-volt appliances. Economically, the best they expect from this change is to break even. Nevertheless the endeavor is worthwhile, because they feel they are doing something to help save our planet. Their motivation is spiritual more than economic; they are committed to eco-spiritual living. In this way they are leading by example, proclaiming their values for others to notice and perhaps follow. Even if no one should imitate them, they have the satisfaction of living according to their convictions and of knowing that their contribution does help.

WHAT ONE PERSON CAN DO

The new creation, according to biblical imagery, is manifest first in the lives of individual human beings and in their relationships. "For anyone who is in Christ, there is a new creation: the old order is gone and a new being is there to see" (2 Cor 5:17). Individual conversion—a personal change of mind and heart—affects those closest to the individual: "the new being is there to see." As more and more people adopt eco-spiritual living, the new creation slowly expands to global dimensions, because the individual is part of a worldwide community.

This transformed and reconciled community includes not only other human beings but also the non-human world, the cosmos which is beloved of God (Jn 3:16). With the earth-community God has made an everlasting covenant, first under the sign of the rainbow (Gen 9:13) and then in the blood of Christ under the sign of the cross (Mt 26:28–29). God's purpose in creating this world is to demonstrate divine love and so to elicit, in return, a free response of love from humanity on behalf of all creation.

Like all spiritual paths, eco-spirituality aims at growth in personal integration and loving concern for others, leading to union with God who is enduring love. Because the individual who is committed to eco-spiritual living belongs to the world community, his or her style of life contributes to the global transformation which we call the new creation: full spiritual and ecological integrity. The eternal plan of God, imprinted in the cosmos, imposes a goal on us all, and that goal is to become a new creation, united in peace and love.

Eco-spirituality cherishes the hope that this goal is attainable by God's help and by the generous efforts of many like-minded individuals. The lives of the saints illustrate the power that becomes available when people yield themselves totally to God's plan. St. Peter Claver (1580–1654) offered himself as a servant of the Africans who were transported to Cartagena, Colombia as slaves. Claver is said to have given hope and religious solace to more than 300,000 slaves before he was thirty-five. In our own time, Mother Teresa of Calcutta has touched the hearts and lives of thousands and has established a religious order that is bringing healing to thousands more throughout the world.

The impetus of eco-spirituality is one of loving service to the needy and care for all creation, as exemplified in the life of St. Francis of Assisi, the patron saint of those who promote ecology. The dynamic of love usually finds expression in hands-on activity, but not exclusively so. We venerate St. Thérèse of Lisieux (1873–1897) as co-patron of missionaries although she was a cloistered Carmelite nun; by God's grace, her brief, hidden life of love and prayer was efficacious in bringing help to people she would never meet. Blessed Gabriella Sagheddu (1914–1939) is regarded as a patron saint of ecumenism because she offered her life for Christian unity. Gabriella's silent, loving union with God as she lay dying from tuberculosis in her Trappistine monastery has helped to strengthen the movement toward the unity of all Christian churches.

Prayer is undoubtedly part of Christian eco-spiritual living. The new creation, like the first creation, is God's doing, and the ones who lose themselves in contemplative wonder at the mystery of God's eternal plan are cooperating intimately with the work of God. Not only action but also devotion and contemplative prayer help to advance "the plan of the one who guides all things as he decides by his own will" (Eph 1:11).

When the disciples of Jesus begged him to teach them how to pray, he gave them a prayer containing the petition, "Your will be done on earth as in heaven" (Mt 6:10). This short phrase is a guideline for eco-spiritual living. Earth is to be valued and reverenced insofar as God's will is carried out on earth as it is in heaven. The purpose of all our prayer and activity is to bring ourselves and the whole earth into creative harmony with the will of God. The more we accomplish God's will, God's plan for creation, the closer we come to the final transfiguration when God will be "all in all" (1 Cor 15:28). The Lord's Prayer could well be our daily prayer for harmony, justice, healing, and peace on earth as in heaven.

Getting Involved

Eco-spiritual living springs from a conversion of attitudes and values. Earlier chapters of this book have presented the new way of thinking which leads to a change of attitudes and values. This final chapter offers practical suggestions for living in harmony both with God and with our total human and non-human environment. We will indicate opportunities for choices that reflect our faith in God and our concern for God's creation.

Eco-spirituality is manifested in responsible eco-spiritual living. It is pharisaical to promote an abstract environmental reform without changing our own personal habits of excessive consumption and wastefulness. The first step in changing the world commences with our personal style of life. The place to begin is not with the rain forests in far-away Brazil but in one's own back yard.

Getting involved means creatively doing whatever we can do in our particular situation to bring our style of life into balance with the earth. Somehow we shall have to break free from the tyranny of advertising, and change our habits of impulse buying and throwing away. We might resolve to stop littering, or begin picking up other people's litter. We might plant a tree. We might boycott the products of industries that cause pollution. By writing letters to our representatives in government, we can support helpful programs and selectively discourage whatever may be ecologically damaging.

The United Nations Environment Programme (UNEP) offers a useful pamphlet called "Personal Action Guide for the Earth." Dozens of suggestions are given for individual practices in the areas of food, energy, water use, avoiding toxic substances, and recycling.[1] Another booklet of useful suggestions is published by The Earth Works Group, *50 Simple Things You Can Do To Save the Earth*.[2] Simple things such as substituting compact florescents for traditional light bulbs or putting a displacement device in the toilet tank can add up to significant savings in resources. The final seven suggestions, for the truly committed, involve slightly more elaborate practices such as composting organic waste for mulch.

Environmental action groups offer further opportunities for involvement. Group meetings provide members with mutual support and encouragement, and generate new ideas for fighting specific problems. Organizations like the Sierra Club, the Isaak Walton League, and the Audubon Society have a long history of environmental service. New organizations spring up to meet specific needs.

Among the numerous newer groups is the Green Movement. In Germany and other European countries, the Greens are a thriving political party. U.S. Greens, established in 1984, have held several national gatherings to formulate a

Green platform or program, mapping goals, principles, and policies that are environmentally friendly. Specific Green values include personal and global responsibility, non-violence, grassroots democracy, and respect for diversity. Spirituality has a role in the Green process, to fill the void of alienation in human hearts and to bring us "to our center, back into balance with ourselves and our community."[3]

An area of environmental and personal importance which is within each one's control is one's diet. So personal is this area, and often so emotionally laden, that individual diversity must be respected; each one has his or her own unique biochemical makeup. Eco-spiritual living bases diet-choices on knowledge of sound nutritional guidelines, and recognizes the impact of these choices on personal well-being, as well as on others who suffer hunger, and on the environment.

A diet that reduces the intake of fat and cholesterol from animal products is a diet that conserves environmental resources and benefits health. If the corn and grains fed to animals could be eaten directly by human beings, millions of starving people could be fed. According to Lester Brown of the Overseas Development Council: ". . . if Americans were to reduce their meat consumption by only 10%, it would free over 12 million tons of grain annually for human consumption."[4]

Eating lower on the food chain, which means eating more grains, vegetables and fruits than animal products, would be a healthier diet for many people. An editorial in *The Journal of the American Medical Association* said in 1961: "A vegetarian diet can prevent 97% of our coronary occlusions."[5] Both the lacto-ovo vegetarian diet, which permits milk products and eggs at times, and the pure vegetarian diet provide adequate high-quality protein for endurance, stamina, and strength.[6] Albert Schweitzer, who lived vigorously to the age of ninety, became a vegetarian for ethical reasons connected with his reverence for life: "He could no longer bear," he explained, "to eat anything that had been alive."[7] Henry David Thoreau, a vegetarian except when it came to fish, ventured the opinion that the trend toward vegetarianism "is a part of the destiny of the human race, in its gradual improvement."[8]

SUSTAINABLE STYLES OF LIFE

A shift to eco-spiritual living is a shift to a style of life that is sustainable far into the future on our bounteous but limited planet. Exploitation and waste are not sustainable indefinitely. A sustainable style of life, for the individual and for the larger community, will use chiefly the renewable resources of the environment, while non-renewable resources will be used sparingly and conserved for future generations.

If manufactured goods were designed to be more durable and if distribution could somehow be more equitable, there could be an increase in the quality of life for a large percentage of the world's population. A smaller percentage would be called upon, by considerations of justice and love if not self-interest, to accept a lower standard of living. Philosopher Ivan Illich explains in an interview the requirements of sustainability:

> Sustainability without development, or subsistence, is simply living within the limits of genuinely basic needs. Shelter, food, education, community, and personal intimacy can all be met within this framework.[9]

Simplified Living

Mohandas Gandhi, the saintly champion of non-violence, used to urge people: "Live simply, so that others might simply live." Simplicity need not be taken to Gandhi's ascetical extreme—going barefoot and clad in a homespun dhoti—but will entail moderation in the use of material goods. If we have what is sufficient for our needs, and only what is sufficient, then perhaps all people may have what they need. The planet is capable of sustaining its growing human population, but not at a level of luxury or wastefulness.

"With respect to luxuries and comforts," says Henry David Thoreau, "the wisest have ever lived a more simple and meager life than the poor."[10] Thoreau insists on this theme: "Simplicity, simplicity, simplicity!"[11] He learned, from his two-year experience of living in a cabin built by himself in the woods beside Walden Pond, how to be content with "the necessaries of life."[12] Raising most of his food in his vegetable garden, Thoreau had no problem supporting himself and abundant time left over for his studies and meditations. "I am convinced, both by faith and experience, that to maintain one's self on this earth is not a hardship but a pastime, if we will live simply and wisely."[13]

Thoreau's idea of living simply does not imply destitution or total deprivation. He went to Walden seeking to savor life in all its depth, to live deliberately and sturdily, to "suck out all the marrow of life."[14] The best way to accomplish this intention, he discovered, was "to make my life of equal simplicity, and I may say innocence, with nature herself."[15]

The simplicity of nature springs from its being nothing but itself. Similarly, a simple, uncluttered style of life springs from a strong sense of who we are as the image and likeness of God, loved to the depths of our being and sustained in existence from moment to moment by our creator. There is no need to seek security from a multitude of perishable possessions when we fully accept our dependence on God. Do not worry, says Jesus:

Do not say, "What are we to eat? What are we to drink? What are we to wear?" It is the Gentiles who set their hearts on all these things. Your heavenly Father knows you need them all. Set your hearts on his kingdom first, and on God's saving justice, and all these other things will be given you as well (Mt 6:31–33).

Simple trust in God's providence empowers us to live in the truth of reality as it is in the present moment. At the same time this simple trust does not entitle us to be spendthrifts, but obliges us to respect the material goods that we use and to value all things as gifts of God.

A spirit of simplicity is careful to reuse or repair an article where possible, or else recycle it. Most cities and towns have collection centers for recyclable material. The more demand there is for recycled goods, such as paper, the more will be supplied. Some industries, including chemical companies, are supporting the trend to recycle, and are finding it good for business.[16] The Worldwatch Institute foresees many countries moving, during the 1990s, toward "comprehensive, systematic recycling of metal, glass, paper and other materials, beginning with source separation at the consumer level."[17]

Appropriate Technologies

A sustainable style of life does not demand the complete dismantling of modern civilization in order to replace it with some utopian, pre-technological paradise. There is no going back. Yet the way forward does not have to be more of the same spiraling, hi-tech development. Alternative technologies—already available but not widely known—are more "appropriate to the conditions of operation and to the operators, and more congenial to the environment, than is much of the sophisticated technology of modern industry."[18] For example, solar box cookers in which the temperature reaches 250 degrees Fahrenheit are an alternative technology for areas where firewood is scarce. For transportation needs, renewable fuels such as ethanol and methanol, especially when produced from biomass, are viable alternatives to fossil fuels.

Agriculture has become a large scale, highly mechanized industry, dependent on chemical pesticides and fertilizers. An alternative suggested by Thomas Berry is to move "away from monocultural, high-energy, petrochemical techniques to more emphasis on organic processes, mixed crops, local markets, permacultures, and year-round food production in solar-heated bioshelters."[19] Appropriate, low-input sustainable agriculture can be nearly as productive as hi-tech farming practices, without hazard to the food or damage to the biosphere. Partly or totally organic farms cooperate with nature as an ally instead of attempting to conquer and control nature by chemical means.[20]

For some individuals, vegetables raised in their own garden provide an abundant source of safe and nourishing food. Gardeners soon discover that their work is soothing to the spirit as well as productive. Even in cities, people who are serious about gardening have found creative ways of growing food; their personal satisfaction is as valuable as their small harvest.

Conversion of Heart

The changes in understanding and behavior that characterize eco-spiritual living will not come about without a profound change of values, a conversion of heart. Habits of consuming have to be replaced by habits of conserving. There will be no modification of consumer demands until there is a conversion of consumers' hearts. Eco-spirituality contributes to this transformation of heart by encouraging people to understand the issues and seek to know and do God's will with boundless trust in the creator's guiding plan for all creation.

Ours is the generation that must begin shifting gears and moving toward an equitable and sustainable style of living if we desire to leave a civilization of any quality for those who come after us to enjoy. Future generations have as much right as we have to benefit from earth's resources and to find inspiration in its overwhelming beauty. We hold the planet in trust for all who will follow us in the succeeding millennia.

Such considerations imply that we are to think not only of ourselves and our personal comfort and convenience, but also of others and of the whole earth. The international community is called to forgive past grievances and devise new forms of cooperation for the benefit of all. Our challenge is to satisfy the legitimate needs of all, rather than the insatiable desires and cravings of a relative few. In this decisive decade, the decade of the environment, humanity must rediscover how to "live lightly on the earth" (the phrase is poet Gary Snyder's).

Changes of this magnitude do not come easily and must be motivated by the deepest spiritual incentives or by sheer desire for survival as a species. One researcher who made a painstaking study of the greenhouse effect was motivated to live more simply when he understood the potential consequences for future generations. He and his wife resolved to give up long vacation trips in the car, to keep their house at 55 degrees, to raise more of their own food and shop only once a month. Even more difficult were the choices they made about family planning.[21] They are trying to take personal responsibility for their style of life in consideration of others who have a right to live on this planet now and in the future. They realize that the world they grew up in—the great American dream world—is no longer the reality we are dealing with today.

The need for a new vision of reality is particularly great among those who are accustomed to abundance and who can afford a life of luxury. In spite of their good will, they are simply not psychologically or socially free to embrace a new style of life. Intercessory prayer for the grace of their conversion relies on God's grace to soften their hardened hearts so that they may "change their ways and be healed" (Is 6:10).

Eco-spirituality may also help such people to see, as eco-economist Jack Wikstrom says, that "the well-being of humankind depends on our achieving increasingly greater harmony with environment—other people, other life forms and things."[22] In addition to prayer and proclaiming our vision of a sustainable style of life, it will be helpful to point to actual models of successful eco-spiritual living.

MODELS OF ECO-SPIRITUAL LIVING

Models or examples are useful to demonstrate that eco-spiritual living is not simply an admirable ideal but one that has been tested for a long period of time by individuals and by communities. These people have lived the ideal without, perhaps, knowing that they did so and without calling it "eco-spiritual living."

Models are proposed not in order to be slavishly imitated but as sources of inspiration and encouragement. They show us, for instance, that it is indeed possible to be happy with fewer material goods. People have lived and are living happy and fulfilled lives that are deliberately simple, deliberately restrained. Their goal is a quality style of life based on cooperative relationships, appreciation of nature, and cele-

bration of the spirit, not on high productivity and high
consumption.

These innovative models are found in rural settings predominantly. Viable urban models are needed because more
than seventy percent of us live in cities.[23] As it is, the rural
models present us with solid alternatives to increasing ur-
banization and unbridled development. We notice that the
tendency is toward scaled-down institutions, empowerment
of men and women on the grass-roots level, reliance on the
energy resources of the region, and ecologically sound methods of agriculture and waste disposal.

These vital communities, fed by a network of creative
educators, become valuable support groups providing a
framework in which individuals can renew their personal
and ecological vision. As these models of eco-spiritual living
become more widely known and imitated, they may become
a leaven in the larger society, gradually spreading their spiritual influence in a culture dedicated to gross materialism.

Native Americans

American Indians developed sustainable ways of living
on this continent millennia before the invasion of Europeans. The country, it is true, was immense, and the Indian
population was relatively small. They lacked firearms and
chain saws. Still, their harmony with the land is impressive;
they learned how to use creatively the available resources
without depleting them. In their simple style of life they
found genuine security and happiness.

The Koyukon-Athabascan Indians are an eminent example, a tribe that has survived and thrived for perhaps 10,000
years in a territory that is both limited in natural resources
and physically challenging.[24] Koyukons today number
around two thousand, dwelling in eleven villages along the
Koyukuk River in central Alaska, just south of the Arctic

Circle. They have adopted the English language and certain useful consumer goods—store-bought clothing, aluminum boats with outboards, snowmobiles, chain saws, rifles, shotguns—but they also retain their musical Koyukon language and many of their ancient traditions.

In recent decades the Koyukons have accepted Christianity, without abandoning their ancestral mythology which gives special honor to ravens. The Great Raven is venerated as the creator who made the world and watches over it through the eyes of the numerous black ravens that circle endlessly in the clear Alaskan skies.

According to Koyukon beliefs, everything in nature—animals, plants, river, snow and ice, moon and stars—is animated by a spirit that makes it aware and sensitive. Animals can understand human voices, even words spoken in a house in the village. It is dangerous to speak disrespectfully of any animal; bad luck may follow in the form of poor hunting, sickness, and accidents. Reverence extends to the way animals are butchered and the way their remains are disposed of; the hide of a moose's head is returned to the forest and hung on a tree, not thrown away.

Moose, bear and fish are staples of the Koyukon diet, since the climate does not favor agriculture. Animals allow themselves to be caught or shot only by hunters who are respectful. Each spring the King Salmons decide whether or not to swim into the Koyukon nets, be caught, be hung up to dry, and be eaten the following winter. The favor of the animals is called "luck." Luck is more than good fortune; it is a state of grace that is won and maintained by attitudes of reverence and humility toward nature, and constant gratitude for nature's bounty. A successful hunter will attribute his achievement to luck, not to his own skill in setting snares for beaver under the ice or his ability to locate the snow-covered den of a black bear. He will say, "I'm not a good hunter, just lucky." By this humility the hunter pleases the animals and keeps up his good luck.

Between the Koyukons and their harsh land there is an intimacy, a reciprocity of care whereby each looks out for the other. The Koyukons live by eating the living spirits of animals and plants, so that the circle of life remains unbroken although altered in form. Thus there is a single, living, harmoniously interrelated community comprising humans, non-human creatures, and the earth itself. This vision of the world is functional for all concerned. The land of the Koyukon, after millennia of use, is still vital and unspoiled, able to sustain its vigorous population indefinitely.

From these and other native Americans who are the original inhabitants of this continent, we can learn how to balance our needs with the needs of the whole earth. From their mystical sense of a spiritual presence in all beings, we can learn to reverence one another and reverence nature. Their willingness to share food generously with one another can inspire us to do the same. The wisdom possessed by American Indians may yet be crucial for the future of our continent. As Thomas Berry says:

> Survival in the future will likely depend more on our learning from the Indian than the Indian's learning from us. In some ultimate sense we need their mythic capacity for relating to this continent more than they need our capacity for mechanistic exploitation of the continent.[25]

Religious Communities

Those who join religious communities are usually attracted by a religious ideal or by a charismatic leader who promises to show them how to live creatively and peacefully. These communities seek harmony with God and with each another, and generally achieve a harmonious relationship with nature as well.

(1) Benedictine and Cistercian monasteries have a tradition of being largely self-sufficient. The sixth century *Rule of St. Benedict* directed: "The monastery should, if possible, be so constructed that within it all necessities, such as water, mill and garden are contained, and the various crafts are practiced."[26] The Cistercians, in their search for solitude, often settled in marshy lands near rivers. They drained these swamps, which were sometimes malarial, and transformed them into productive farmland. Waterwheels put the river to work, while windmills provided another source of energy. Today monasteries find it difficult to be totally self-sufficient; most earn their living through specialized agriculture or small industries, or by providing academic or pastoral services.

The Benedictine concept of stability makes it possible for monastics to put down roots in the place where they dwell; they develop a close, harmonious contact with their environment, with its seasons and rhythms, its native plants, birds and animals. The monastic practice of silence helps people be attuned to their surroundings, and to listen for God who speaks in all creation. Silence is often the most appropriate response to mystery, to the sacred. The sloweddown pace of life in a monastery, punctuated by frequent prayer services, creates an atmosphere of tranquility that is healing and relaxing. In a monastery the ordinary tasks of daily living are esteemed; material things are esteemed; time is esteemed, not wasted. All these are gifts of God to be gratefully and creatively used.

The Benedictine-Cistercian way of life unfolds under the twin precepts of work and prayer. Work is understood in a broad sense including both intellectual and physical labor. The result of this fortunate combination of theoretical and practical skills, along with prayerful openness to the divine presence in creation, has been fruitful for a multitude of people throughout the centuries. Fruitful too, and well cared for, is the land surrounding these monasteries, especially where organic methods of farming and pest management are in use.[27]

(2) Zen Buddhism teaches the interdependence of all beings. The separate existence of humans—separate from one another and from nature—is considered an illusion, although the illusion is functional on an everyday level. Techniques of meditation and mindfulness help bring the practitioner to a calm centeredness in which the oneness of all reality can be experienced.

Although Zen is not a religion in the strict sense, the Zen Center in California has some similarities to monastic religious communities. The daily practice of group zazen is essential to this style of life. Zen principles and ideals are embodied in the ordinary activities of the men, women, and children who belong to this community. They seek for balance, integration, discipline, and beauty in everyday life.

Zen Center, California, is located in several places: the mountain retreat at Tassajara, the farm at Green Gulch, and various businesses and services in San Francisco. The farm is cultivated by hand and by horse. Workshops, such as the bakery, use appropriate technologies, relying as much as possible on renewable energy. Zen Center not only supports itself but reaches out to serve others who are not part of the Center. The Center welcomes dialogue with other cultures on subjects such as non-violence and alternative styles of life that are friendly to the environment. Zen Center has been called "a new form of community that is uniquely adapted to the economic, political and ecological needs of contemporary America."[28]

(3) On the shore of a bay in the Madawaska River in

Ontario, Canada stands the headquarters of Madonna House, a Roman Catholic training center for men and women founded by Catherine de Hueck Doherty in 1947. Membership totaled one hundred and seventy-three in 1989. Staff workers make a lifetime commitment to serving one another and the poor, in poverty, chastity, and obedience, either in Ontario or at one of the mission houses throughout the world. Every year thousands of pilgrims partake of their hospitality and of their reverent, Byzantine-influenced worship services.

Manual labor is a major element of the day at Madonna House. One of the directors writes of "the constant pressure of building, feeding, creating beauty, sewing, repairing, providing maintenance, caring for the land and the animals."[29] The community begs for its needs and for the poor, but they also attempt to feed themselves by running a widespread and diversified farm, using draft horses to pull cultivators, weeding the vegetable gardens by hand, making their own cheese, butter, bread, and maple syrup.

Madonna House is conscious of carrying out a mission of "universal restoration" in Christ (Acts 3:21), a restoration that extends not only to people and things but to the land itself. The land is restored by people living in deliberate simplicity and in close connection with the seasonal rhythms of nature. The Madonna House "Little Mandate" instructs the members: "Do little things exceedingly well for love of me (Christ)." Whether it is washing dishes, doing calligraphy for a publication, sorting donated clothing for the poor, or harvesting and milling trees for lumber, Madonna House staff-workers are putting love and care into their efforts for the restoration of all things. The Madonna House way of life is busy and at times burdensome, but it is also deeply healing and restorative, powerfully beneficial for the members, for others, and for the earth.

Earth Island Centers

These non-profit centers—two dozen of them through-out the United States—are dedicated to research and education in ecology. They adapt principles of ecology to the local environment, the wildlife, the forests and lakes, and the farmland. In the interests of a sustainable economy, they develop systems of renewable energy. As training centers, they accept apprentices for work/study programs.

For example, at the fifteen-hundred acre Meadowcreek Farm in Fox, Arkansas, both staff and students have daily, hands-on, educational opportunities for farm work. The farm is an integrative laboratory, where ecology interacts with economics, and principles of organic agriculture are tested at the marketplace. Classroom learning is completed by practice in the corn fields and the barns. Students acquire both professional competence and commitment to earth values. They care about nature and are educated to interact with nature professionally and compassionately. Leadership development programs sharpen managerial skills and ecological literacy. Meadowcreek Farm, like other Earth Island Centers, strives to be "an interdisciplinary laboratory where learning, grounded in experience, can take place."[30]

Genesis Farm

Begun in 1980 on a one hundred and forty acre site in northwestern New Jersey, Genesis Farm is a Catholic-sponsored learning center directed by Dominican Sister Miriam McGillis.[31] The goal is to integrate spirituality and ecological sensitivity.

The staff and students of Genesis Farm try to overcome the alienation of western society from the earth. They explicitly incorporate the new story of the universe, as sketched in Chapter 1, at the basis of their thinking and their vision of the future. In addition they draw from three distinct sources of inspiration:

(1) The natural world considered as a living organism. The water cycles, the soil and atmosphere, the plants and living animals—all these are a sacred book revealing something about the creator. Nature reveals God as loving, healing, nourishing, and protective of life. Nature shows that God desires diversity but also communion. At Genesis Farm the solstices and equinoxes are celebrated with appropriate festivals.

(2) The legacy of native Americans, especially the Delaware Indians who occupied the area surrounding Genesis Farm. The Indians, with their sense of nature as sacred, scarcely altered their physical environment in the course of thousands of years.

(3) All religious traditions, especially Judeo-Christian and the Celtic. These traditions are tapped for their wisdom and experience relating to ecological wholeness.

Another objective is to rediscover and appreciate the surrounding bioregion, that community of living and non-living beings sustaining itself in a particular geographical area. As a means of helping people reconnect with the earth, Genesis Farm teaches such skills as pottery, macrobiotic cooking, organic gardening, permaculture design (integration of human and natural systems), and the identification of edible or medicinal plants.

Still another objective is to link their local community with the global community as part of a movement toward a new, more secure and pluralistic world order. They attempt to go beyond personal and national selfishness in order to be concerned about the needs of people throughout the world. This global social consciousness complements their ecological concerns.

Genesis Farm offers its students opportunities for study,

work, prayer and celebration. The program is designed to open new ways of thinking about ourselves and our culture. The attempt is to redefine our relationship with all creation and its creator.

COMMITMENT TO ECO-SPIRITUALITY

In this chapter we have seen how eco-spirituality might be lived by ordinary people in a variety of contexts. Eco-spiritual living begins on the level of one's own individual life, by making hard choices for conservation and simplicity. What can I do, with the help of God's grace, to reform my outlook and my consumer behavior? How can I personally move toward a more reverent, caring, healthy, and environmentally friendly life? From this commitment to conversion and holiness, eco-spirituality may expand in a global direction as described in Chapter 6, but the new creation begins in the individual human heart. As St. Paul says, ". . . what matters is a new creation" (Gal 6:15).

Eco-spirituality is a strongly incarnational spirituality that embodies its ideals in actual daily living. Like every form of spirituality, eco-spirituality builds on a foundation of loving faith and hope, trusting the basic goodness of the material creation, trusting the sacrament of matter to bring us, all together, into the realm of the Spirit who makes all things new (see Chapters 2, 3 and 5).

Above all, eco-spirituality trusts God the creator, because the new creation, like the first creation, is God's work. "It is all God's work. . . . I mean, God was in Christ reconciling the world to himself" (2 Cor 5:18). We do not yet see with much clarity the shape of the new creation because we are too close to it, we are in process with it. What we see more clearly is the cosmic catastrophe that lies ahead if humanity chooses to continue on its present, irresponsible course. With that prospect, we also see our need for the mercy of God.

Happily, God abounds in mercy and love. God who so loved the cosmos that "he gave his only Son" loves and cares for it still (Jn 3:16). Eco-spirituality, relying on the divine compassion, is rightly hopeful about humanity changing its course during this "Decade of the Environment."

Further grounds for hope have been suggested by philosopher David Ehrenfeld in a slightly different context. He points to the resilience of the human spirit and its ability to resist the current of the times if it so wishes. Ehrenfeld speaks of "the capacity of men and women to stand alone, triumphant, in simplicity, independent of the constructions and devices of society and the plans of other people."[32]

We know, of course, from our considerations in Chapter 4, that we never stand totally alone in this interdependent universe. The stance we take as individuals, in favor of the new creation, will have a greater or lesser effect on those closest to us and on the entire cosmos. The human spirit has, in addition, the capacity to cooperate with the creator and with others, to forgive, to find life-giving meaning even in negative situations, and to maintain a sense of humor. Eco-spirituality is optimistic that, at last, humanity will begin to let itself be guided by the wisdom of the Spirit who renews the face of the earth.

APPENDIX

❧

Resources for Eco-Spirituality

In addition to the groups already noted in Chapter 7, the following list of names and addresses may be helpful for anyone wishing to pursue the course of action recommended in that chapter. Some of these associations stress the ecological more than the spiritual, but most of them attempt to integrate the spiritual dimension into their ecological agenda. The order of listing is alphabetical, not by relative importance.

Co-op America.   Provides Alternative Marketplace Catalogs which list socially responsible businesses selling everything from food to magazines. Sends to American business the message that "It pays to care" (about environmental quality, about justice in the workplace, about integrity of products).

> Co-op America
> 2100 M Street, N.W., Suite 310
> Washington, DC 20063

Earthcommunity Center.   Expands the familiar agenda of social justice and peacemaking to include the earth itself. The place of the human community is within, not above, the larger earth community. Director Jane Blewett travels to give workshops or retreats in order to awaken a sense of responsibility toward earth.

Earthcommunity Center
15726 Ashland Drive
Laurel, MD 20707

The Eleventh Commandment Fellowship. The Eleventh Commandment is: "The earth is the Lord's and the fullness thereof; thou shall not despoil the earth, nor destroy the life thereon." The Fellowship offers a slide show package, and a listing of ecologically harmful products in daily use, with recommended alternatives.

The Eleventh Commandment Fellowship
P.O.B. 14667
San Francisco, CA 94114

Living Water Contemplative Center. A place to help us experience the spirit in nature by teaching solitude, silence, and patient waiting, in the uniquely unspoiled and stark environment of the Greater Yellowstone area.

Living Water Contemplative Center
John B. Kirsch
P.O.B. 997
West Yellowstone, MT 59758

National Catholic Rural Life Conference. Brings together Catholic social teaching and issues of food, environment, agriculture, rural life, and simple living. Newsletter, "Common Ground," nine times a year.

National Catholic Rural Life Conference
4625 Beaver Avenue
Des Moines, IA 50310

North American Conference on Christianity and Ecology (NACCE). Founded in 1986 by Al Fritch and others who are concerned about developing a Christian environmental ethic. Seeks to involve Christian clergy and churches, as the

best organized sector of society, in a common project of healing the earth. Sponsors conferences on Christian ecology
and publishes a quarterly called *Firmament*.

> North American Conference on Christianity
> and Ecology
> 161 E. Front Street, Ste. 200
> Traverse City, MI 49684

North American Coalition on Religion and Ecology
(NACRE). Founded in 1989 by Donald B. Conroy, this
group co-sponsored an Inter-Continental Conference on
Caring for Creation in 1990. The purpose is to involve people of all religious backgrounds in the campaign to save our
planet and its life systems. Helps parish congregations become centers for ecological renewal.

> North American Coalition on Religion and Ecology
> 5 Thomas Circle, N.W.
> Washington, DC 20005

Shomrei Adamahd (Guardians of the Earth). A project of
The Federation of Reconstructionist Congregations and Ha-
vurot to foster seder celebrations of nature holidays such as
the Jewish New Year of the Trees and to study and restore
the environment according to guidelines from Jewish
tradition.

> Shomrei Adamahd
> Ellen Bernstein
> Church Road and Greenwood Avenue
> Wyncote, PA 19095

Notes

CHAPTER 1

1. W.C. Vanderworth, ed., *Indian Oratory* (University of Oklahoma Press, 1971), p. 121. On the authorship of the alleged letter of Chief Seattle to President Pierce, see Eugene C. Hargrove, "Editorial," *Environmental Ethics*, vol. 11, no. 3 (Fall 1989), pp. 195–196.

2. Charles Darwin, *Descent of Man*, 2nd ed. (1874; rpt. New York: Burt, n.d.), p. 188, quoted in Robert Augros and George Stanciu, *The New Biology* (Boston: Shambhala, 1988), p. 217. The following quotations from Darwin are also found in *The New Biology*.

3. Walter Abbott and Joseph Gallagher, eds. and trans., *The Documents of Vatican II* (New York: America Press, 1966), "The Church Today" (*Gaudium et spes*), no. 5, p. 204.

4. Thomas à Kempis, *The Imitation of Christ* (Garden City: Image Books, 1955), I:1, p. 32. Subsequent references are to book and chapter.

5. R.A. Knox, *Enthusiasm* (Oxford: Clarendon Press, 1950), p. 213, quoting Abercrombie, *The Origins of Jansenism*.

6. Ibid. p. 213 quoting Frances Martin, *Angelique Arnauld*.

7. Jerome Besoigne, *Principes de la perfection*, pp. 97–98, as quoted by Pierre Pourrat, *Christian Spirituality* (Westminster: The Newman Press, 1955), Vol. IV, p. 270.

8. R.A. Knox, op. cit. p. 203.

9. Pierre Pourrat, op. cit. p. 20.

10. See Pierre Pourrat, op. cit. p. 268.

11. R.A. Knox, op. cit. p. 212.

12. William Wordsworth, "Tintern Abbey," from Louis Untermeyer, ed., *A Treasury of Great Poems, English and American* (New York: Simon and Schuster, 1942), p. 640.

13. See Ronald W. Clark, *Einstein, The Life and Times* (New York: Avon Books, 1971), pp. 269–270.

14. Peter Michelmore, "Einstein, Albert," *The New Encyclopaedia Britannica* (1974), Macropaedia 6, p. 513.

15. Alan Lightman, *Time Travel and Papa Joe's Pipe* (New York: Penguin Books, 1984), p. 60.

16. See Paul Davies, *God and the New Physics* (New York: Simon and Schuster, 1983), p. 187.

17. Ibid. p. 198.

18. Ken Wilber, ed., *Quantum Questions* (Boston: Shambhala, 1985), p. 114.

19. Ibid. p. 61.

CHAPTER 2

1. See Karl Rahner, *Foundations of Christian Faith* (New York: Seabury, 1978), pp. 14–23, 31–35.

2. W.H. Gardner, ed., *Poems and Prose of Gerard Manley Hopkins* (Harmondsworth: Penguin Books, 1953), "The Starlight Night," p. 27.

3. Talmud as quoted by Ilya Prigogine and Isabelle Stengers, *Order Out of Chaos* (Boulder and London: Shambhala, 1984), p. 313.

4. See St. Thomas Aquinas, *Summa Theologiae*, Part One, Question 47, Article 1: "The whole universe together participates the divine goodness more perfectly and represents it better than any single creature whatever."

5. Theophilus of Antioch, *Letter to Autolycus*, ch. 2, no. 3, in M.J. Rouet de Journel, *Enchiridion Patristicum*, 4th & 5th ed. (Friburg: Herder and Co., 1922), p. 72, no. 177.

6. St. Cyril of Alexandria, *Commentary on John*, Bk. II, ch. 9, in M.J. Rouet de Journel, op. cit. p. 665, no. 2119.

7. St. Athanasius, *Defence of the Nicene Definition (De Decretis)*, ch. 3, no. 11, in M.J. Rouet de Journel, op. cit. p. 262, no. 754.

8. St. Hilary, *On the Trinity*, Bk. II, no. 5, in M.J. Rouet de Journel, op. cit. p. 317, no. 860.

9. "You were more inward than the most inward place of my heart and loftier than the highest," says St. Augustine, *The Confessions of St. Augustine*, trans. F.J. Sheed (New York: Sheed and Ward, 1943), Bk. 3, ch. 6, p. 48.

10. Miriam Pollard, *The Listening God* (Wilmington: Michael Glazier, 1989), p. 40.

11. T.C. McLuhan, ed., *Touch the Earth: A Self-Portrait of Indian Existence* (New York: Pocket Books, 1972), p. 37. See also Matthew Fox, *Original Blessing* (Santa Fe: Bear and Co., 1983), Theme 6 "Panentheism: Experiencing the Diaphanous and Transparent God," pp. 88–92.

12. See Kenneth L. Schmitz, "Concrete Presence," *Communio* (Fall 1987), pp. 313–314. Note that reality remains mysterious even as it manifests its mystery. Things and people are always more than they appear to be. Like the kachina masks used in Hopi initiation rituals, reality masks or conceals God at the same time as it reveals God. See Belden C. Lane, *Landscapes of the Sacred* (Mahwah: Paulist Press, 1988), pp. 41–42.

13. See Walter M. Abbott and Joseph Gallagher, *The Documents of Vatican II* (New York: America Press, 1966), "The Church Today" no. 22, p. 220: "The truth is that only in the mystery of the incarnate Word does the mystery of man take on light."

14. See William R. Crockett, *Eucharist: Symbol of Transformation* (New York: Pueblo Publishing Company, 1989), pp. 248, 256, 262.

15. Fiona Macleod, *Where the Forest Murmurs*, quoted by Aaron Sussman and Ruth Goode, *Walking* (New York: Simon and Schuster, 1967), p. 365.

16. Theodore W. Kraus, "Led Back into the Wilderness," *Creation*, vol. 5, no. 2 (May/June 1989), p. 40.

17. St. Augustine, *The City of God*, trans. Marcus Dods (New York: The Modern Library, 1950), Bk. 22, no. 24, p. 851.

18. "Embers, Stars, and Beer Cans, An Interview with Era-

zim Kohak by David M. Denny," *Desert Call*, vol. 25, no. 2 (Summer 1990), p. 13.

CHAPTER 3

1. Edgar D. Mitchell, "Outer Space to Inner Space: An Astronaut's Odyssey," *Saturday Review*, February 22, 1975, p. 20.

2. See J. Lemaitre, "Nature et Vie Spirituelle," *Dictionnaire de Spiritualité* II, 1806ff. A thirteenth century theologian, Alan of Lille, expressed the common view in a clever Latin triplet: *"Omnis mundi creatura/quasi liber et pictura/nobis est et speculum"* (Every creature of the world is like a book for us, or a picture, or a mirror).

3. Irenaeus of Lyons, *Against Heresies*, from *Office of Readings* (Boston: St. Paul Editions, 1983), p. 164.

4. Nicodemos of the Holy Mountain, *A Handbook of Spiritual Counsel*, trans. Peter Chamberas (New York: Paulist Press, 1989), p. 202.

5. Thomas Merton, "Is the Contemplative Life Finished?" *Contemplation in a World of Action* (Garden City: Image Books, 1973), pp. 363–364.

6. Evagrius Ponticus, *Praktikos*, trans. John Eudes Bamberger (Spencer: Cistercian Publications, 1970), p. 39, no. 92.

7. Ibid. *Chapters on Prayer*, p. 63, no. 51.

8. *The Confessions of St. Augustine*, trans. F.J. Sheed (New York: Sheed and Ward, 1943), Bk. 9, ch. 10, pp. 200–201.

9. D.W. Wallace-Hadrill, *The Greek Patristic View of Nature* (New York: Barnes & Noble, 1968), p. 128.

10. St. Basil, *Hexaemeron*, trans. Blomfield Jackson, *A Select Library of Nicene and Post-Nicene Fathers, Second Series*, vol. VIII (Grand Rapids: Wm. B. Eerdmans Publishing Company, 1952), 5:2, p. 76. See also 6:1, p. 82.

11. See Susan Power Bratton, "Oaks, Wolves and Love: Celtic Monks and Northern Forests," *Journal of Forest History* (January 1989), p. 9.

12. *Life of St. Columban* (PL 87:1028, no. 30).

13. Mary Aileen Schmiel, "Exploring Celtic Spiritual Lega-

cies," in *Western Spirituality,* ed. by Matthew Fox (Santa Fe: Bear and Company, 1981), p. 175.

14. "The Hermit's Song," trans. Kuuno Meyer, quoted in Susan Power Bratton, op. cit. p. 14.

15. *The Letters of Bernard of Clairvaux,* trans. Bruno Scott James (London: Burns & Oates, 1953), [106] 107, p. 156.

16. Martinus Cawley, trans., *Bernard of Clairvaux: Early Biographies,* vol. 1 (Lafayette: Guadalupe Translations, 1990), p. 31 (PL 185:240).

17. Hugh of St. Victor, *Seven Books of Didactic Instruction,* Bk. 7, ch. 3 (PL 176:814).

18. Julien Green, *God's Fool: The Life and Times of St. Francis of Assisi* (San Francisco: Harper & Row, 1985), pp. 254–259.

19. Bonaventure, *The Soul's Journey Into God,* trans. Ewert Cousins (New York: Paulist Press, 1978), ch. 1, no. 15, p. 67. See also ch. 2, no. 12, p. 76: "The creatures of the sense world signify the invisible attributes of God."

20. Bonaventure, *Collationes in Hexaemeron,* ed. by F.M. Delorme (Quaracchi: Collegium S. Bonaventurae, 1934), xii:15.

21. *Meister Eckhart,* trans. Raymond Blakney (New York: Harper and Brothers, 1941), Sermon *"Quasi stella matutina,"* p. 222.

22. *The Spiritual Exercises of St. Ignatius,* trans. Anthony Mottola (Garden City: Image Books, 1964), p. 104. See also p. 57.

23. One could list Robert Southwell, Gerard Manley Hopkins, Teilhard de Chardin, Anthony de Mello, Karl Rahner, and Albert Fritsch. See Peter Schineller, "St. Ignatius and Creation-Centred Spirituality," *The Way,* vol. 29, no. 1 (January 1989), pp. 46–59.

24. St. Teresa of Avila, *The Book of Her Life,* trans. Kieran Kavanaugh and Otilio Rodriguez (Washington, D.C.: ICS Publications, 1976), ch. 9, no. 5, p. 72.

25. J.P. de Caussade, *Abandonment to Divine Providence,* trans. E.J. Strickland (3rd English ed.; St. Louis: B. Herder, n.d.), Bk. 1, ch. 1, no. 3, p. 5.

26. Ibid. Bk. 1, ch. 2, no. 2, p. 18.

27. Pierre Pourrat, *Christian Spirituality* (Westminster: The Newman Press, 1955), Vol. 4, p. 381.

28. *The Autobiography of St. Therese of Lisieux*, trans. John Clarke (Washington, D.C.: ICS Publications, 1976), ch. 1, p. 14.

29. Joseph Mary Plunkett, "I See His Blood Upon the Rose," Thomas Walsh, ed., *The Catholic Anthology: The World's Great Catholic Poetry*, 1st rev. ed. (New York: Macmillan, 1941), p. 428.

30. Pope John Paul II, *Apostolic Letter to the Youth of the World*, March 31, 1985, no. 14, *The Pope Speaks*, vol. 30, no. 3 (1985), p. 219.

31. Frank Whaling, ed., *John and Charles Wesley* (New York: Paulist Press, 1981), p. 302.

32. *The Confessions of Jacob Boehme*, in Anne Fremantle, ed., *The Protestant Mystics* (New York: Mentor Books, 1964), p. 45.

33. Thomas Traherne, *Poems, Centuries and Three Thanksgivings*, ed. Ann Ridler (London: Oxford University Press, 1966), The Second Century, no. 97, p. 259.

34. Ibid. The First Century, no. 37, p. 180.

35. Ibid. The Second Century, no. 67, p. 244.

36. Henry Vaughan, "The Retreat," in Anne Fremantle, ed., *The Protestant Mystics*, p. 70.

37. Ibid. p. 71.

38. Cotton Mather, *The Christian Philosopher*, as quoted by Belden C. Lane, *Landscapes of the Sacred* (Mahwah: Paulist Press, 1988), p. 104.

39. Jonathan Edwards, *Personal Narrative*, in Anne Fremantle, ed., *The Protestant Mystics*, p. 126.

40. *Autobiography of Jacob Bower* in Anne Fremantle, ed., *The Protestant Mystics*, p. 183.

41. Henry David Thoreau, *Walden and Civil Disobedience* (New York: Perennial Classics, 1965), p. 83. See pp. 67, 235, 71, 227 for the earlier quotations.

42. John Muir, *John of the Mountains*, quoted in Richard Cartwright Austin, *Baptized into Wilderness* (Atlanta: John Knox Press, 1987), p. 92.

43. Ibid. p. 12.

44. Ibid. p. 13.

45. Thomas Kelly, *A Testament of Devotion,* quoted in Dorothy Phillips et al., eds., *The Choice Is Always Ours* (San Francisco: Harper & Row, 1975), p. 436.

46. Thomas Kelly, op. cit., quoted in Philip Joranson and Ken Butigan, *The Cry of the Environment* (Santa Fe: Bear and Co., 1984), p. 348.

47. See the anthology *Words From the Land,* ed. by Stephen Trimble (Salt Lake City: Peregrine Smith Books, 1989).

48. Pope John Paul II, *Message for the Celebration of the World Day of Peace* (January 1, 1990), no. 14.

49. As quoted by Olivier Clement, *Sources: Les mystiques chrétiens des origines* (Paris: Editions Stock, 1982), p. 193.

50. Simone Weil, *Gravity and Grace* (London: Routledge, 1952), p. 138.

CHAPTER 4

1. Ken Wilber, *The Holographic Paradigm and Other Paradoxes* (Berkeley: Shambhala Publications, 1988), p. 250.

2. Jay B. McDaniel, *Earth, Sky, Gods and Mortals* (Mystic: Twenty-Third Publications, 1990), p. 99.

3. See Mary Ann Finch, "Befriending the Body," *The Way,* vol. 29:1 (January 1989), pp. 60–67; Ann Wilson, "Holistic Spirituality," *Spirituality Today,* vol. 40:3 (Autumn 1988), pp. 208–219.

4. See Thomas Berry, "Bioregions: The Context of Reinhabiting the Earth," *Riverdale Papers* X (November 1984), p. 4.

5. Jeremy Rifkin, *Declaration of a Heretic* (Boston: Routledge and Kegan Paul, 1985), p. 108.

6. David Ehrenfeld, *The Arrogance of Humanism* (New York: Oxford University Press, 1978), p. 105.

7. Ken Wilber, *The Holographic Paradigm and Other Paradoxes* (Berkeley: Shambhala Publications, 1988), p. 215.

8. Vincent Rossi, "The Eleventh Commandment: Toward an Ethic of Ecology," *Epiphany Journal* 6:1 (Fall 1985), p. 29; see also the quotation from John Scotus Eriugena in Chapter 1.

9. Br. Aidan (Athanasius Hart), "Where the River Flows," *Epiphany Journal* 9:2 (Winter 1989), p. 35.

10. Rabindranath Tagore, *Gitanjali* (New York: Collier Books, 1971), p. 85.

11. Thomas Berry, "The Dynamics of the Future: Reflections on the Earth Process—Its Newly Emerging Phase," *Riverdale Papers on the Earth Community* (Special Collection), p. 17.

12. M. Weiss, *The Bible From Within* as quoted by Mark S. Smith, *The Psalms: The Divine Journey* (New York: Paulist Press, 1987), p. 22.

13. Thomas Merton, *A Vow of Conversation: Journals 1964–1965* (New York: Farrar, Straus, Giroux, 1988), p. 156.

14. Thomas Aquinas, *Summa Theologica*, trans. Fathers of the English Dominican Province (New York: Benziger Brothers, 1947), Vol. One, First Part, Q. 47, Art. 2, p. 246.

15. Louis Agassiz as quoted by Ilya Prigogine and Isabelle Stengers, *Order Out of Chaos* (Boulder and London: Shambhala, 1984), p. 197.

16. John A. Livingston, *The Fallacy of Wildlife Conservation* (Toronto: McClelland and Stewart, 1981), p. 36.

17. The marvelous order and harmony of all creatures "is called the sympathy and the 'sympnoia'—the mutual 'co-breathing' of nature," according to the eighteenth-century Athonite monk, St. Nicodemus of the Holy Mountain, *A Handbook of Spiritual Counsel* (New York: Paulist Press, 1989), p. 198.

18. Ilya Prigogine and Isabelle Stengers, *Order Out of Chaos* (Boulder and London: Shambhala, 1984), p. 287.

19. Francis Thompson, "Ode to the Setting Sun," ed. Terence L. Connolly, *Poems of Francis Thompson* (rev. ed., New York: Appleton-Century Company, 1941), p. 89.

20. Sean McDonagh, *To Care for the Earth: A Call to a New Theology* (Santa Fe: Bear & Co., 1986), p. 119.

21. Benedicta Ward, ed. and trans., *The Lives of the Desert Fathers* (Kalamazoo: Cistercian Publications, 1981), p. 110, no. 15.

22. John Moschus, *Spiritual Meadow*, ch. 107, J.P. Migne, *Patrologiae Latinae*, Tomus 74:172–173. For other monastic examples see Susan Power Bratton, "The Original Desert Solitaire: Early Christian Monasticism and Wilderness," *Environmental Ethics*, vol. 10, no. 1 (Spring 1988), pp. 31–53.

23. Lawrence Cunningham, ed., *Brother Francis* (Huntington: Our Sunday Visitor, 1972), p. 99. By tracing the literary history of wolves, especially the Penitent Wolf motif, in Christian hagiography, Edward A. Armstrong demonstrates that the legend of the wolf of Gubbio is a parable portraying "reconciliation by virtue of holy power between nature and [humankind]." See Edward A. Armstrong, *Saint Francis: Nature Mystic* (Berkeley: University of California Press, 1973), p. 202.

24. Jay B. McDaniel, *Earth, Sky, Gods & Mortals* (Mystic: Twenty-Third Publications, 1990), p. 19.

25. Jeremy Rifkin, *Confessions of a Heretic* (Boston: Routledge and Kegan Paul, 1985), p. 98.

26. William Sloan Coffin, *Once to Every Man* (New York: Atheneum, 1977), p. 339.

27. Because ecological problems often affect more than one nation, Pope John Paul, without calling for a world government, points to the necessity of "a more internationally coordinated approach to the management of the earth's goods" (*Message for the Celebration of the World Day of Peace*, January 1, 1990, no. 9). An option favored by ecologist Gary Coates is: "A global federation of relatively small-scale, self-reliant ecocommunities, operating on the renewable energy flows of sun, wind, and water and integrated into ecologically and socially stable bioregional economies." See Gary J. Coates, ed., *Resettling America: Energy, Ecology & Community* (Andover: Brick House Publishing, 1981), p. 547.

28. Jay B. McDaniel, *Earth, Sky, Gods and Mortals* (Mystic: Twenty-Third Publications, 1990), p. 29.

CHAPTER 5

1. Albert Schweitzer as quoted by James Brabazon, *Albert Schweitzer: A Biography* (New York: G.P. Putnam's Sons, 1975), p. 258.

2. Marion Mill Preminger, "I Will Never See His Grave: Memories of Albert Schweitzer," *Fellowship in Prayer*, vol. 40, no. 6 (December 1989), p. 50.

3. James Brabazon, op. cit. p. 345.

4. Ibid. p. 254.

5. "Preserving and Cherishing the Earth: An Appeal for Joint Commitment in Religion and Science," as quoted in an editorial in *America*, vol. 162, no. 5 (February 10, 1990), p. 116.

6. James Brabazon, op. cit. p. 52.

7. Paul Davies, *God and the New Physics* (New York: Simon and Schuster, 1983), p. 159.

8. See Karl Rahner, *Theological Investigations*, vol. 6, *Concerning Vatican Council II* (New York: Crossroad, 1982), pp. 190, 247; vol. 9, *Writings of 1965-1967 I* (New York: Crossroad, 1985), p. 188; *Foundations of Christian Faith* (New York: Crossroad, 1982), p. 447.

9. Richard A. McCormick, *Health and Medicine in the Catholic Tradition* (New York: Crossroad, 1957), p. 148.

10. James Brabazon, op. cit. p. 404.

11. T.C. McLuhan, ed., *Touch the Earth: A Self-Portrait of Indian Existence* (New York: Pocket Books, 1972), p. 22.

12. Ibid. p. 56.

13. Rex Taloosi as quoted by Demetria Martinez, "Indians Fight Burial of Radioactive Waste," *National Catholic Reporter*, June 30, 1989, p. 12.

14. T.C. McLuhan, ed., op. cit. p. 170.

15. See Thomas Berry, *The Dream of the Earth* (San Francisco: Sierra Club Books, 1988), chap. 14, "The Historical Role of the American Indian," pp. 180-193.

16. Jacques Ellul, *The New Demons* (New York: Seabury Press, 1975), p. 73.

17. Hong Kong Diocese, *Sunday Examiner*, vol. 44, no. 9 (March 2, 1990), p. 6.

18. Jeremy Rifkin, *Declaration of a Heretic* (Boston: Routeledge and Kegan Paul, 1985), p. 84.

19. Robert Brungs, *You See Lights Breaking Upon Us* (St. Louis: Versa Press, 1989), p. 136.

20. Timothy Fry, ed., *RB 1980* (Collegeville: Liturgical Press, 1981), ch. 31, p. 229. See Charles Cummings, "Benedictine Reverence Revisited," *American Benedictine Review*, 41:3 (1990), p. 325ff.

21. Helen Bacovcin, trans., *The Way of a Pilgrim* (Garden City: Image Books, 1978), p. 34.

22. Fyodor Dostoeyevsky, *The Brothers Karamazov*, trans. Constance Garnett (New York: Random House Modern Library, 1950), p. 337.

23. See Gary J. Coates, *Resettling America: Energy, Ecology and Community* (Andover: Brick House Publishing, 1981), p. 539.

24. Frank Waters, *Book of the Hopi* (New York: Penguin Books, 1977), p. 195.

CHAPTER 6

1. Howard Heiner, "Restoring the Land," *Creation*, vol. 5, no. 2 (March/April 1990), p. 21. According to Matthew Fox, "The killing of Mother Earth in our time is the number one ethical, spiritual, and human issue of our planet"—*The Coming of the Cosmic Christ* (San Francisco: Harper & Row, 1988), p. 144.

2. Information from Marian Chetow in a lecture on "The Impasse in Solid Waste Management," at Chautauqua Institute, Chautauqua, New York, 1989 (on cassette recording). See also Ronald Searle, "Down in the Dumps," *Smithsonian* 21:1 (April 1990), pp. 146–159.

3. Thomas Berry, "Technology and the Nation-State in the Ecological Age," *Riverdale Papers* VIII, p. 4.

4. Philip Sherrard, "Confronting the Ecological Challenge," *Epiphany Journal* X:3 (Spring 1990), p. 14.

5. Sean McDonagh, *To Care for the Earth: A Call to a New Theology* (Santa Fe: Bear and Company, 1986), p. 178.

6. William E. Rees, "Towards an Ecological Economics," *Green Letter* (Winter 1989), p. 16.

7. Lester R. Brown, ed., *State of the World* 1990 (New York: W.W. Norton & Company, 1990), p. 190.

8. John Paul II, *On Social Concerns* (Boston: Daughters of St. Paul, 1988), no. 28.

9. Stanley Samuel Harakas, "Ecological Reflections in Contemporary Orthodox Thought in Greece," *Epiphany Journal* X:3 (Spring 1990), p. 54.

10. Gale Warner, "Ecology is the Contemporary Religion," *Earth Island Journal* (Winter 1988–89), p. 28.

11. These paths are described in Matthew Fox, *Original Blessing* (Santa Fe: Bear and Company, 1983).

12. Matthew Fox, *The Coming of the Cosmic Christ* (San Francisco: Harper & Row, 1989), p. 82.

13. Ibid. p. 83.

14. The book of Genesis is not in conflict with the new story of the universe as told below in Chapter 1, as long as the literary genre of the biblical narrative is taken into account. The biblical language is mythopoeic and does not contradict the findings of astrophysics and archeology.

15. See Richard E. Leakey, *The Making of Mankind* (London: Michael Joseph Limited, 1981), pp. 242, 223, 230, 221.

16. John L. McKenzie, "God and Nature in the Old Testament," *The Catholic Biblical Quarterly*, vol. XIV (1952), p. 136.

17. For a persuasive presentation of Jesus as an "ecological figure" and of the ecological motif in the entire Bible, see H. Paul Santmire, *The Travail of Nature* (Philadelphia: Fortress Press, 1985), pp. 189–218.

18. Elizabeth J. Canham reviewing St. Athanasius, *On the Incarnation*, in *Weavings* II:6 (November/December 1987), p. 42.

19. St. Athanasius, *Discourse Against the Pagans*, 42–43 as found in *The Office of Readings* (Boston: Daughters of St. Paul, 1983), p. 170.

20. Maximus the Confessor, *Ambigua*, as quoted by Issa J. Khalil, "For the Transfiguration of Nature: Ecology and Theology," *Epiphany Journal*, vol. 10, no. 3 (Spring 1990), p. 35.

21. Isaac the Syrian, *Mystical Treatises*, trans. A.J. Wensinck (Amsterdam, 1923; Wiesbaden reprint 1969), vol. II, ch. 74, p. 341.

22. Vladimir Lossky, *The Mystical Theology of the Eastern Church* (London: James Clarke and Co., 1973), p. 111.

23. St. Theodore of Studios, *Homileia 3 in Nativitatem Beatae Virginis Mariae* 4–7, as found in *A Word in Season*, ed. by Friends of Henry Ashworth (Still River: St. Bede's Publications, 1981), p. 112.

24. See Jane Blewett, "Social Justice and Creation Spirituality," *The Way*, vol. 29, no. 1 (January 1989), pp. 13–25.

25. *World Charter for Nature*, General Assembly Resolution 37/7 (28 October 1982), *United Nations Yearbook 1982*, pp. 1023–1026. The record shows that one hundred and eleven member states voted for this charter, eighteen abstained, and one voted against it. The sole negative vote was cast by the United States, for two reasons: the language of the charter should be more precise; the charter should not put individual persons under obligation to uphold the charter.

26. "Ten Affirmations of Faith," *One World*, no. 155 (May 1990), p. 11.

27. "For the Transfiguration of Nature," *Epiphany Journal*, vol. 10, no. 3 (Spring 1990), p. 73.

28. Ibid. p. 73.

29. Stanley S. Harakas, "Ecological Reflections in Contemporary Orthodox Thought in Greece," *Epiphany Journal*, vol. 10, no. 3 (Spring 1990), p. 46.

30. John Paul II, *On Social Concerns*, nos. 30, 32 (Boston: St. Paul Books, 1988).

31. Ibid. no. 34.

32. Ibid. no. 26.

33. John Paul II, "Peace with God the Creator, Peace with All of Creation," World Day of Peace, January 1, 1990, no. 5.

34. Ibid. nos. 15, 7.

35. Ibid. nos. 8, 9.

36. Ibid. no. 13.

37. *The Assisi Declarations* (Gland: WWF International, 1986), p. 12.

38. Ibid. p. 31.

39. Ibid. p. 23.

40. Ibid. p. 6.

41. Ibid. pp. 18–19.

42. *The Managua Declaration*, no. 2, as found in *Earth Island Journal*, vol. 5, no. 1 (Winter 1990), p. 53.

43. *Economic Justice for All* (Washington, D.C.: U.S. Catholic Conference, 1986), no. 12, p. 6.

44. Catholic Bishops of the Philippines, "What Is Happening to Our Beautiful Land," approved at Tagaytay, January 29, 1988

(mimeographed copy), pp. 1–10. Subsequent quotations are from the same source.

45. Bishops of Lombardy, "Ecology," trans. Howard Limoli et al. (San Francisco: North American Conference on Christianity and Ecology, 1989), p. 1.

46. Ibid. p. 9.

47. Jane Blewett, "Rediscovering Earth Can Be Awe-Inspiring," *National Catholic Reporter*, vol. 26, no. 19 (March 2, 1990), p. 2.

CHAPTER 7

1. *Personal Action Guide For the Earth* is available from Friends of the U.N., 730 Arizona Ave., Suite 329, Santa Monica, CA 90401.

2. The Earth Works Group, *50 Simple Things You Can Do To Save the Earth* (Berkeley: Earthworks Press, 1989).

3. Green Committees of Correspondence Green Program, *Green Letter Greenes Times*, vol. 6, no. 3 (Winter 1990), p. 72. Information on U.S. Greens is available from GCoC Clearinghouse, P.O.B. 30208, Kansas City, MO 64112. *Green Letter* is published at: P.O.B. 14141, San Francisco, CA 94114.

4. Quoted by John Robbins, *Diet for a New America* (Walpole: Stillpoint Publishing, 1987), p. 352.

5. Quoted by John Robbins, *ibid.* p. 247.

6. Ibid. pp. 157, 179.

7. James Brabazon, *Albert Schweitzer: A Biography* (New York: G.P. Putnam's Sons, 1975), p. 463.

8. Henry David Thoreau, *Walden and Civil Disobedience* (New York: Harper & Row, 1965), p. 161.

9. Interview with Ivan Illich by the editors of *New Perspectives Quarterly*, reprinted as "The Shadow Our Future Throws," *Earth Ethics*, vol. 1, no. 2 (Winter 1990), p. 5.

10. Henry David Thoreau, *Walden and Civil Disobedience* (New York: Harper & Row, 1965), p. 11.

11. Ibid. p. 67.

12. Ibid. p. 9.

13. Ibid. p. 52.

14. Ibid. p. 67.

15. Ibid. p. 65.

16. See the 110 page special advertising section in *Business Week*, no. 3165 (June 18, 1990), pp. 47–157.

17. Lester R. Brown, ed., *State of the World 1990* (New York: W.W. Norton and Company, 1990), p. 182.

18. E.F. Schumacher, *Small Is Beautiful* (New York: Harper & Row, 1975), p. 179.

19. Thomas Berry, *The Dream of the Earth* (San Francisco: Sierra Club Books, 1988), p. 63.

20. See Jeanne McDermott, "Some Heartland Farmers Just Say No to Chemicals," *Smithsonian*, vol. 21, no. 1 (April 1990), pp. 114–127. A supportive network of organic farms is coordinated by: Rodale Institute, 222 Main Street, Emmaus, PA 18098.

21. Bill McKibben, *The End of Nature* (New York: Random House, 1989), p. 188.

22. Jack Wikstrom, "Linking Inventory and Analysis in an Ecosystem Context," an unpublished paper presented at the Conference on Global Natural Resource Monitoring and Assessments, in Naples, Italy, 1989, p. 3.

23. Richard Register, president of Urban Ecology, Inc., organized the First International Eco-Cities Conference in Berkeley, California, March 29–April 1, 1990.

24. All data about the Koyukons comes from *Make Prayers to the Raven*, a series of six television programs produced by KUAC-TV at the University of Alaska, Fairbanks, 1987. Richard K. Nelson, writer and associate producer of the series, is the author of a book by the same title (University of Chicago Press, 1983).

25. Thomas Berry, *The Dream of the Earth* (San Francisco: Sierra Club Books, 1988), p. 190. Carl Jung once said: "The American, on account of the fact that he lives on virgin soil, has the Red Indian in him. The Red man, even if he has never seen one . . . [has] gotten into the American and you will realize that he belongs to a partly colored nation." C.G. Jung, "The Symbolic Life," as quoted by John A. Sanford, *Dreams and Healing* (Mahwah: Paulist Press, 1978), p. 83.

26. Timothy Fry, ed., *RB 1980: The Rule of St. Benedict* (Collegeville: The Liturgical Press, 1981), ch. 66, p. 289.

27. For the history of one monastery's initial attempt to free itself from agribusiness methods, see Brother Mary Kevin, OCSO, "Monks and Agribusiness," *Catholic Rural Life* (October 1980), pp. 21–26. On the loss of monastic farms in the context of global agricultural problems, see Terrence Kardong, "Monks and the Land," *Cistercian Studies*, 1983:2, pp. 135–148.

28. Gary J. Coates, *Resettling America: Energy, Ecology and Community* (Andover: Brick House Publishing, 1981), p. 117.

29. Jean Fox, "One Man's Scrap, Another Man's Gold," *Restoration*, vol. 43, no. 5 (May–June 1990), p. 8. Madonna House is at Combermere, ON K0J 1L0.

30. Sam Passmore and Pat Muntz, "Education: From Ivory Tower to Open Field," *Earth Island Journal*, vol. 4, no. 1 (Winter 1988–89), p. 49. Meadowcreek Farm is at Fox, AR 72051.

31. All information is taken from Sr. Miriam T. McGillis, "Genesis Farm Experiment Seeks Transforming Vision in Values, Community," *Catholic Rural Life*, vol. 38, no. 2 (June 1988), pp. 9–11. Genesis Farm may be addressed at P.O.B. 622, Blairstown, NJ 07825.

32. David Ehrenfeld, *The Arrogance of Humanism* (New York: Oxford University Press, 1978), p. 267.